Gladly Learn, Gladly Teach

Gladly Learn, Gladly Teach

Living Out One's Calling in the 21st-Century Academy

Edited by
John Marson Dunaway

Mercer University Press
Macon, Georgia
2005

ISBN 0-86554-965-6
MUP/P309

© 2005 Mercer University Press
1400 Coleman Avenue
Macon, Georgia 31207
All rights reserved

First Edition.

∞The paper used in this publication meets the minimum requirements
of American National Standard for Information
Sciences—Permanence of Paper for Printed Library Materials, ANSI
Z39.48-1992.

Library of Congress Cataloging-in-Publication Data

Gladly learn, gladly teach : living out one's calling in the 21st-century
academy / edited by John Marson Dunaway.— 1st ed.
p. cm.
Includes bibliographical references and index.
ISBN 0-86554-965-6 (pbk. : alk. paper)
1. Christian education—Philosophy. 2. Vocation—Christianity. 3. College
teachers—Religious life. I. Dunaway, John M., 1945-
BV1464.G53 2005
261.5—dc22
2005002833

Table of Contents

This book is dedicated to

Thomas J. Glennon
&
Margaret Dee Bratcher

Uncommon visionary leaders of the Commons

Acknowledgments

First, I wish to thank the Lilly Foundation, without whose financial support and imaginative and resourceful leadership this project probably never would have been conceived. Next, I acknowledge the inspiration and support of Thomas J. Glennon, who in writing our Lilly grant application cast the vision of the Commons, and Margaret Dee Bratcher, who so ably led the Commons and was an unfailingly consistent enabler and encourager in the planning and editing of this volume.

My contributors, both from Mercer and from around the country, were admirably cooperative and their essays were a true joy to read. I count myself fortunate to have my name associated with their superb work. Wilfred C. Platt, Coordinator of the Commons Fellows, was an invaluable editorial consultant, and the Fellows themselves (Larry L. McSwain, Richard F. Wilson, Douglas Thompson, Fred W. Bongiovanni, Andrew Silver, Peter C. Brown, Gregory Domin, J. Colin Harris, W. Loyd Allen, and D. Micah Hester) also provided significant help in the early brainstorming stage, as well as guidance throughout the editorial process.

Credit is also due to the participants in the 2003-2004 Commons Colloquium, where most of these essays originated, both formal responders and those (students, staff, and faculty alike) who participated in the discussions from the audience. Let the conversation gladly continue.

Finally, I am happy to acknowledge the contributions of my wife Trish, who always shares my burdens and provides the creativity I so often lack but so highly value.

Introduction

John Marson Dunaway
Mercer University

"The university is a clear-cut fulcrum with which to move the world.... More potently than by any other means, change the university and you change the world."[1] So wrote Charles Habib Malik in 1982. Yet just a few years later Harvard President Derek Bok, in his report to the Harvard Board of Overseers, wrote: "Professors are trained to transmit knowledge and skills within their chosen discipline, not to help students become more mature, morally perceptive human beings."[2] In light of Bok's statement, should it come as a surprise that the corporate executives who were responsible for the staggering moral failures of recent years (Enron, WorldCom, Arthur Andersen) were trained at our elite universities, most of which were founded upon ideals such as *Lux et veritas* (Yale), *In Deo speramus* (Brown), and *Eruditio et religio* (Duke)? The contemporary cultural crisis, if it is to be addressed at all, must be engaged not just by intellectuals but by thinkers with a conscience formed in the crucible of faith and learning. It is because of the urgency of this need that the present volume has been compiled.

In recent years American higher education has witnessed an increasingly penetrating conversation centering upon the question of how faith and learning should be related. The dialogue has been buttressed by organizations such as the Lilly Foundation, which has disbursed millions of dollars to eighty-eight universities and colleges across the nation engaged in the Project for the Theological Exploration of Vocation. InterVarsity Fellowship and Christian Leadership Ministries have sponsored huge conferences and published numerous articles and books on the topic.

Many scholars have contended for decades that American higher education in the twentieth century was characterized primarily by a steady trend toward secularization.[3] Whether one subscribes to the secularization

---

[1] Charles Habib Malik, *A Christian Critique of the University* (Waterloo, Ontario: North Waterloo Academic Press, 1987) 100-101.

[2] Quoted in Mark R. Schwehn, *Exiles from Eden: Religion and the Academic Vocation in America* (New York: Oxford University Press, 1993) 3.

[3] James T. Burtchaell, *The Dying of the Light: The Disengagement of Colleges and Universities from Their Christian Churches* (Grand Rapids: Eerdmans, 1998).

xii

thesis or not, however, all those who value the unique contribution of religious faith to higher learning should be encouraged by the growing literature on faith and learning. It is indeed a thrilling time to be engaged in the conversation.

Chaucer enthusiasts will recognize that the title of the present volume is borrowed from the Prologue to the *Canterbury Tales* and its description of the Clerk, who is a model for all who aspire to be good teachers:

> A CLERK ther was of Oxenford also,
> That unto logyk hadde longe ygo.
> ...Sownynge in moral vertu was his speche,
> And *gladly wolde he lerne and gladly teche.*

One might comment on several of the Clerk's attributes and their importance in the making of an effective teacher, but brevity is one of those, so we shall confine ourselves to the two traits mentioned in this volume's title. It is instructive that Chaucer's picture of the ideal teacher places primary emphasis upon the priority of learning before teaching. Good teachers must always begin as good learners. One of the first lessons in the apprenticeship of novice instructors is that one learns much more in the process of teaching—and in that of the requisite preparation—than in solitary study. I am equally happy with the element of gladness, which Chaucer emphasizes by repetition, in his description. Indeed, we professors must first become and always remain learners, nay glad learners, in order to be effective teachers. For such would be the case of all whose vocation in academe might fit Frederick Buechner's definition of "the place where your deep gladness meets the world's deep need."[4]

The present volume of essays originated in a six-part colloquium during academic year 2003-2004, sponsored by the Mercer Commons, a Center for Faith, Learning and Vocation at Mercer University. The Commons was created through a generous grant from the Lilly Foundation, which also made the publication of this collection possible. Faculty and students from across the ten colleges and schools of the university gathered on six occasions and were led by a panel of three speakers per session in reflecting on the theme: "Gladly Learn and Gladly Teach: Living Out One's Calling in a Baptist University." The result of the colloquium was what one

---

[4] Frederick Buechner, *Wishful Thinking: A Seeker's ABC* (San Francisco: HarperSanFrancisco, 1993), 119.

prominent Mercer professor of religion called "the most engaging conversation on this campus on the proper relationship of faith and learning in recent memory."

A committee of the Commons Fellows selected the best six essays from the colloquium and invited five prominent scholars from other American universities to contribute to the anthology, in hopes of producing a collection whose applicability would expand far beyond the particularities of Mercer, a Baptist-affiliated comprehensive university located in Macon, Georgia.

That, in brief, is the story of the genesis of this book. It has been a delightful learning experience for me to serve as its editor. My contributors have been admirably cooperative, and I consider their essays to be practical, enlightening, creative, well written, and eminently sensitive to the mystery that surrounds the elusive goal of excellence in teaching wedded to genuine spiritual wisdom. The Mercer essays (chapters one through six) have been placed at the beginning and are arranged chronologically, since at least two of them build upon their predecessors in the colloquium, thus giving a sense of the shape that the conversation on faith and learning has been taking here on the Mercer campus. Chapters seven through eleven were written by scholars from across the country and broaden the conversation, reflecting the compelling ongoing dialogue in the national context.

The authors are teacher-scholars who genuinely seek to live out the sometimes-competing vocations of professor and believer. They represent a wide diversity of academic fields and faith perspectives: not just theology, but law, political science, teacher education, philosophy, foreign language, and literature; not just Protestant, but Catholic and Jewish, evangelical and moderate. Though most of them teach in church-related institutions, three are administrators, one being a dean in a secular university. All contributors not only affirm the need for a clear theological vision on which to base institutional and pedagogical planning; they also stress the importance of diversity, pluralism, and true academic freedom. Indeed, they seem to agree that even a responsible church-related liberal arts institution must, of necessity, stress these features in academic life.

The theological positions of these scholars, too, are far from lock-step uniformity. The importance of pluralism and of non-integrative approaches to faith and learning is balanced by calls for being guided by the mind of Christ, rather than the mind of the academy. We believe that readers will be challenged by this diversity of viewpoints to think in new and creative ways about the relationship of faith and learning that will fit the history, character, and identity of their specific institutions.

Mercer President R. Kirby Godsey sets the tone for the conversation in a meditation on the importance of understanding the art of teaching as an essentially relational event. Drawing upon Martin Buber's exploration of the I-Thou relationship, he outlines a transformational pedagogy that accords in many ways with Parker Palmer's notion of creating a space for learning in the classroom. It is a space that is not dominated by a dispenser of knowledge ["'Teaching' is not an agent/patient encounter"], but shared by co-learners who respect the sacredness of the distance between each other and between their ideas. Godsey seeks to "rescue the journey of learning" by reminding the teacher of the necessity [again a theme in Palmer] of the inward journey of self-examination: "She must look within to find the Thou that makes it possible to hear the calling to teach." I am reminded, too, of Tolstoy's Ivan Ilyich, who is prevented from apprehending any meaning in his life until, in the face of death, he is finally able to grow still and listen to his own quiet inner voice.

Poet Gordon Johnston responds to Godsey by reminding us that the space for learning is created around a *subject* as the all-important center. Regarding the I-Thou meeting we seek with our students, he reminds us of "what brought the meeting about in the first place, the altar over which student and teacher meet. If that altar is anything but the subject we risk demagoguery, condescension, and profanity." Using the poetic resources of Whitman, Dickinson, and Pattian Rogers, Johnston pursues Godsey's (and Palmer's) inward journey with an even subtler sense of the ever-unfinished project of selfhood.

Philosopher Charlotte Thomas's essay is one of the more profoundly personal reflections upon childhood as the source of experiences of transcendence and the sacred. She brings memories of what French novelist Marcel Proust would have called privileged moments (*moments privilégiés*) together with insights about French medieval architect Abbé Suger, who created a space conducive to the awareness of the sacred in his masterful Basilica of Saint-Denis. It is just this sort of atmosphere, suggests Thomas, that must be fostered in order to arrive at a transformational pedagogy.

In R. Alan Culpepper's essay we find first a handy review of the place of teaching in the biblical tradition, upon which he builds a theology of teaching. For Culpepper, to teach is to awaken, to encourage, to model. It is an exercise in hope in which we must remind ourselves that students can and will be more than they now are. It partakes in creating, it happens in community, and is incarnational and personal. It is a way of helping students write their futures.

Interestingly enough, it is the law professor among our authors who has chosen to address the pedagogy of Jesus' parables. Jack L. Sammons borrows from Paul Ricoeur's thinking about parables and Wittgenstein's notion of discovering "the extraordinary within the ordinary" in an extended reflection upon the biblical story of the Good Samaritan. The art of the teacher as it is modeled by Christ in telling this parable is essentially concerned, Sammons shows, with making the listener understand something he or she really already knows. We may see a certain resemblance here to what Gordon Johnston says in his earlier essay: "By making the familiar strange the poet brings the listener or reader to see the world as it is (or as the poet would have it be) rather than as the reader expects it to be."

The concluding essay from the original Mercer colloquium focuses upon the importance of pluralism, even in a denominational institution. Andrew Silver examines the differences among levels of openness in religious adherents: from exclusivists like Jonathan Edwards, to inclusivists like C. S. Lewis, and finally to pluralists, which is the stance to which he himself has evolved. He argues that for him to answer the question of pluralism in a Baptist university, he has to speak as a Jew, from experience, about what pluralism would mean at a Jewish university, and so he gives examples of what he thinks students at a Jewish university should study about other world religions. "Until we have learned to love other faith traditions and until we learn to see from other perspectives, inclusion remains a judgment made without embrace, without love."

Richard T. Hughes's essay seeks to clarify what is necessary for church-related institutions to become authentically Christian—that is, authentically infused with the spirit of the Gospel, rather than simply maintaining a formal link with a denomination. He takes up some of Silver's themes, emphasizing the importance of diversity, pluralism, and academic freedom for an institution that seeks to be faithful to its faith tradition. And he also speaks of the necessity for administrations, development officers, and governing boards to base their marketing and fund-raising techniques and their governing policies upon the faith perspectives of their founders. "Sanctification *and* justification are the two indispensable poles of the paradox of the Christian gospel, and the two indispensable dimensions of Christian higher education," he says. And a humble awareness of our human limitations and "the frank acceptance of the fact that we are justified not by works or knowledge or wisdom, but by God's infinite grace, should make us cautious about dogmatisms of every kind."

As is fitting for a classically trained literary scholar, David Lyle Jeffrey gives us a rich tapestry of literary sources, from Augustine to Aquinas and Luther, from Shakespeare to Herbert to George Eliot and Frost. His meditation upon calling, buttressed too by his own autobiographical itinerary, comes to center around the necessity for teacher/scholars to work in community. He notes that the rule of St. Benedict provided that "each special calling was still part of an overall calling to a community life which, especially among groups such as the Benedictines, had learning at its core. ... If we do not make time for participation in the lives of others our own best thinking, in the end, is likely to become myopic, perhaps to all but a few, incomprehensible or substantially irrelevant. ... We may be in grave danger of forgetting our calling altogether, having become preoccupied with the means rather than the end, the goal of our vocation. This is really idolatry."

As the lone Roman Catholic contributor to this collection, Jeanne Heffernan provides a somewhat different theological perspective. She begins, as several others in this volume do, with an autobiographical context for her reflections upon the challenge of teaching out of a wholeness of heart, mind, and spirit. Not surprisingly, she makes use of the rich intellectual tradition of Catholic thinkers like Cardinal Newman, Jacques Maritain, and Pope John-Paul II in advocating "an expansive, unified curriculum, grounded in the conviction that approaching life and learning through a dedication to the liberal arts illumined by faith provides the surest initiation into wholeness." She shows how teaching out of wholeness necessarily entails teaching prayerfully. "Placing our common work in the context of prayer is to remind us of the only context that gives our studies their full meaning." For Heffernan, at least, this means starting each class with prayer.

William Hull addresses the voice—or lack thereof—of Baptists in the contemporary faith and learning debate. The relative paucity of distinctly Baptist contributions to the conversation, according to Hull, can largely be attributed to the wars of attrition that have plagued Baptist life during the past few decades. His analysis of the situation is cogent and disturbing. The two specific cases in point that he examines at length (Baylor and Union Universities) amount, he contends, to adaptations of approaches that are not really inspired by a distinctively Baptist concept of higher education. He calls for a fresh start in re-imagining the ideal of the Baptist university. "The denomination, in partnership with its schools, needs to develop a shared vision for higher education that both can enthusiastically support."

The final essay in this anthology is perhaps the most challenging. Mary Poplin's meditations on faith and learning come out of a radical mid-life conversion from secular post-modern intellectualism to biblical faith, a conversion that compelled her to serve "the least of these" in the streets of Calcutta with Mother Teresa. It also compelled her—even though she remained at a secular university—to rebuild her entire pedagogical philosophy by prayerfully seeking the mind of Christ, rather than continuing to labor under the ubiquitous dictates of the mind of the academy. "I need to know that Christ still heals," she writes, "that God speaks in often inexplicable ways, and that we do not live in a purely natural or purely knowable world. I have to remain connected to the miraculous and constantly search for the still small voice or else my faith, my personal growth, and my intellectual work suffer."

The authors of these essays, like a growing number of teacher/scholars across the country, have made a paradigm shift in the model for higher education that they are seeking to embody. They view their work not primarily as a career but as a calling, a way of serving God and humanity in the noblest tradition of Geoffrey Chaucer's Oxford Clerk. They begin in the humility of gladly learning in order to arrive at the goal of gladly and effectively teaching. They enter into the mystery of the I-Thou relationship with their students, attempt to re-present the reality of the subject in a way that will draw out what their students already unconsciously know, and prayerfully approach their duties with a healthy sense of their own limitations. They reach out to a diverse and pluralistic world of colleagues and students, avoiding the intolerance of triumphalism while seeking to remain faithful to the mind of Christ rather than the mind of the secular academy.

These writers do not presume to have found all the definitive answers to the dilemmas of faith and learning. However, they invite the reader's active participation in the ongoing conversation in hopes that these essays will in some small way help us examine with growing insight how we may all come to exert a truly redemptive influence upon contemporary American higher education. Ideas do indeed have consequences, and we all should be reminded of the crucial role we can play in shaping the Augustinian quest of "faith seeking understanding" among the future movers and shakers of our society. In that spirit, let us indeed humbly, faithfully, and gladly live out our calling in the twenty-first century academy.

In Willingham Chapel

For Ben Griffith

An old building, and a classroom dangling off a creaking stairway.
The desks creaked also,
                     the floor complained.
the crippled lectern tottered on its crutch. An old room, yes,
but not entirely dead,
each brittle window enlivening a yellowed page ...

Wordsworth was there, and Dorothy, Coleridge with his tragic teeth,
Peacock and Lamb, Godwin
spouting sedition,
                     portly Mr. Blake in the attic with his angels ...

A quiet man spoke and something woke up in my heart.
Suddenly, I remember,
                     the shy world wanted to talk.

But that was a long while ago,
                     and other than gratitude
so little survives the world's chronic revision—a line, maybe,
from a poem you've forgotten, a nickel
you salvaged from an alley
for luck,
                     a voice that blessed you in passing ...

David Bottoms is Georgia's current poet-laureate, a professor of English at Georgia State University in Atlanta, and a 1971 alumnus of Mercer University. He has graciously granted us permission to re-print here a poem that he wrote in honor of Ben Griffith, who was one of his instructors of English at Mercer. Griffith's classes met in the classroom space of Willingham Chapel, one of the two oldest buildings on Mercer's Macon campus.

CHAPTER ONE

The Higher Calling of the Undergraduate Experience

By R. Kirby Godsey, President
Mercer University

We are born connected and all of us, from our births, become a part of a journey toward becoming more fully human, toward finding the meaning of our particular presence in the world, and even toward hearing what I will refer to as "a calling" that echoes deep within the recesses of each person's life.

Our human journey destines each of us to be a learner. Apart from active and engaged learning, we are mostly like empty clay shells, passively being molded, but unable to speak with a sense of personal authority that springs from within. In our earliest years, our learning is largely unstructured—sounds and sights that find their way into the space we occupy. As we grow, our learning becomes more structured. We begin to be educated more formally.

Our lower education can sometimes seem to become a grand scheme of manipulation. Our structures for learning become increasingly rigid with tables to be memorized and curricula to be mastered. But, in general, we educate for the common good. We set out a common curriculum of history and science and mathematics and literature to serve as the foundation for tutoring young minds.

I have no quarrel, indeed, with the rigorous pursuit of established curricula, except perhaps that they should be more rigorous and less distracted by the paraphernalia of the social context. That is, we at times appear compelled to muddle education with a curriculum that includes such things as instruction in driver's education and sex education, and how to interview for a job. We become preoccupied with offering courses on alcohol abuse and drug abuse and the effective uses of birth control. All of these subjects warrant some attention, no doubt, but I think it is a mistake to presume that everything a youngster needs to know should be taught in the public schools. I say the schools ought to forget teaching driver's education and sex education and how to be a parent. Let the Department of Motor Vehicles or the church or the Wednesday Club or would you even believe the parents teach them how to drive or be a parent or how to make love more effectively. Schools do not really make good surrogate parents.

Education, I believe, is first and foremost about helping to enable every person to become a person, to probe and to exploit his resource bank of talent, and to reconnect, in imaginative and compelling ways, with the world from which he sprang.

This journey of connecting, in my judgment, does not begin by looking outward. I believe that the journey of relating is first and foremost an inward journey. Fostering, inspiring, cajoling, facilitating, and encouraging that journey may be among our highest callings as educators, particularly as educators in an undergraduate context.

The whole struggle of growing through adolescence becomes mostly consumed with understanding ourselves over against parents and friends, finding our place over against established traditions and taboos. Self-preservation usually comes as the first order of business of parents, teaching our young the rules of the road. We teach them the socially acceptable ways to act, to dress, to speak, to wear their hair and to stand in public. We teach them how to belong and how to fit into the social fabric.

And then we send them off to the University for higher education where they may be met more with higher training than higher learning. There our disciplines have multiplied and we are faced with gifted professors who literally know more about their subjects than anyone on earth and their goal often is to recreate their students in their own image.

Here students also enter the world of the core undergraduate experience. In my view, the goal of this common educational experience should be to rescue the journey of learning from an enterprise that produces well-educated students who have never been set free to hear the interior voices that will ultimately tutor them toward a sense of purpose and hope. I believe that it is not enough to produce competent engineers or superb accountants or effective counselors at the bar. The result of such a goal, standing alone, would be to produce practitioners and professionals who are well trained but who have never visited the intersection of who they are and what they do. I regard this intersection of who we are and what we do to be a holy place where one ought to put a stone and build a temple. And if we have not been to that intersection in our lives, we are likely to suffer from a kind of empty careerism that leads inevitably to the traumas of burnout and self-doubt.

The truth is that many, if not most, of our programs of general education are neither general nor educational. They are a set of politically negotiated courses that insure every discipline's turn to "show and tell" in the competition to recruit majors. The field of general education has, in large measure, sacrificed the common learning space to the academic political landscape where elaborate academic duels take place in order to demonstrate academic might. Politics prevail over teaching and learning.

I am reminded that during the Kennedy administration, Arthur Schlesinger left Harvard to accept an appointment in Washington, D.C. When asked why he would leave his prestigious post at Harvard, he replied, "I have decided to leave Harvard and go to Washington in order to get out of politics for a while."

The President of Columbia University was heard to report that academic politics is the most vicious of all politics for two reasons:

—The stakes are so small.
—The people of honor are always outnumbered by the people of principle.

Harland Cleveland, who served as Dean of the Hubert Humphrey Institute at the University of Minnesota, was, back in the turmoil of the Vietnam era, the newly-elected President of the University of Hawaii. When asked why he would go to lead that institution where the turmoil was at its highest—marching and daily protests, often on the verge of violence, he said, "If you are going to have trouble, you might as well have it in good weather."

Well, the weather is frequently stormy for people who are sharing the cause of a common educational core. And the predictions are not for the weather to get much better. Politics will continue to prevail in powerful ways, sometimes even erupting into violent storms. We must work to enable the essential mission of the educational experience not to become lost, amidst the cacophony of disciplinary priorities that consume our universities and their resources.

In all candor, I believe that the most persistent source of our problems may be an undereducated professoriate and the ignorance of people in charge. Esoteric scholarship is better compensated than the scholarship of leading students to probe enduring and thorny issues, even though these issues turn out to shape the human spirit and affect dramatically the wellbeing of human culture. Again, the value and contributions of scholarship should certainly not be diminished. But neither should it be seen as the defining and ultimate issue of the academic enterprise. I actually believe that we would probably do well to require our first- and second-year faculty to participate in a core-learning program. It is very difficult to expect that the teacher who has never made that long and disarming journey inward to find the courage to mentor another in such a journey. The preoccupation with our "discipline-centric" professional careers can become a means of avoiding the inner and more difficult questions that emerge on the human terrain. We define our careers and finally ourselves by the discipline we serve. Take away our disciplines and we have no way to center our lives. The discipline becomes the defining essence of our being here. Take the discipline away and all is emptiness: "Vanity of vanities, all is vanity."

I suspect none of us need look beyond the boundaries of our institution to find clear and tragic examples of colleagues who yearn to recover or to find for the first time a purposefulness about their work. They long for a purpose that they actually bring to their work instead of relying upon the work itself as the sole provider of meaning and purpose. Freedom is hardly something they actually experience—intellectual freedom, yes but the freedom to be, the freedom to reconnect with the inner life has been lost to the shadows, lost in the abyss of "discipline-centric" definitions of what it means to be a teacher.

Teaching without connecting is akin to the breaking of day without the rising of the sun. It is surprising how often the notion of intellectual freedom is used to refer to the right to probe the outer world without encumbrance, yet the same freedom is not claimed to probe the depths of inner experience.

While we might use one of any number of works, let me refer to Martin Buber as a way of framing my point. Actually, I believe that Martin Buber has much to teach us about teaching. The lesson of *I and Thou* is not the lesson of duality. The lesson of *I and Thou* is the lesson of the ultimate power of relatedness. The "I" of the teacher is realized only in meeting the "Thou" of the student. The mantra of teaching should be Buber's affirmation that "all real living is meeting" and where there is no meeting, there may be abstract instruction, we may even find the rigorous but mechanistic training of the mind, but we will find nothing so elegant and engaging as teaching going on. Above all else, teaching is a relational event. And a relational event worthy of the moniker "teaching" is not an agent/patient encounter.

The world we call teaching is a radically different calling. The calling of a teacher is born of the intimate, powerful, and transforming experience of connecting. In Berger's metaphor, the "I" of the teacher cannot be born without the "Thou" of the student.

The recovery of the power of relating, in my view, belongs to the mission of a general education program. A core text such as *I and Thou* becomes a vehicle for navigating the organic cellular structure of teaching and for negotiating the powerful inward journey of learning.

The I-Thou is not the connecting of an "I" and a "Thou." No, the relation is primary. The action is in the hyphen. There is no "I" without the "Thou" and the "Thou" only becomes an "I" in the mutuality of the relational event. If an instructor wishes to become a teacher, she must look within to find the Thou that makes it possible to hear the calling to teach.

I use this reference to suggest that we are all children of relatedness. Our life form itself is an issue of relatedness. When we observe another person, what we really observe is what I have chosen to call a "region of behavior." Something we call a person is actually an extrapolation, an exemplification of certain relationships. It is not the case that we exist and then we relate. Our presence is an expression of our relatedness. Apart from relating, we do not exist. We are nothing. We are not a person in relation, or a person who relates. We do not create relationships.

Relationships create us. A person is a window for seeing and understanding the constellation of relationships that shape the substance of what it means to be a solitary individual. The solitary individual is an abstraction and to regard a solitary "I" as an essential entity is what Alfred North Whitehead would have called "misplaced concreteness."

While the individual, that is, the individual as student or the individual as teacher, should not be seen as the primary unit of reality but more as an extrapolation of reality, the way into this constellation of relationships is more inward than outward. That is to say, we understand the "Thou" component of our being here not by dissecting and analyzing the other over against which we stand, but by having the courage to take the most strenuous and difficult journey into ourselves.

Every journey inward takes us into our essential relatedness. And it is in the inner zone that we are able to catch a glimpse of the connections that create our particular presence. The intersection of those connections also constitutes the substance of what I refer to as our own unique calling. In other words, the only truly unique aspect of our being here, the only individuality we possess is our unduplicated and singular "calling." I use "calling" here in the broadest possible sense. It is a poetic term to refer to a particular and profound intersection of connections that occurs only once in the world. DNA, for example, is an exemplification of that intersection of connections but not an exclusive one. Our relatedness or our peculiar constellation of connections is the only "non-clonable" aspect of our being here. That aspect of our being here called DNA is only one component of our relatedness, albeit a major and defining component of the set of connections that constitute our identity.

In probing the discussions of our relatedness, we can consider several macro levels of human connectedness. Those macro levels include (1) our connections within, our inner relatedness or how we relate to ourselves, (2) how we relate to other people, and (3) exploring our connections with the world.

As individual persons, we are not isolated or independent from the vast universe that embraces us. You and I exist among the stars and this enormous expanding universe of about 15 billion years belongs to the fabric of our interior lives. Any sense that we possess a standing independent of the galaxies is simply mistaken. We are profoundly and inextricably bound up with this universe of light and darkness to which we belong. We belong to its matter and energy and that belonging also teaches us something about our presence here. We are not discrete organisms in the midst of a lifeless, inanimate world. We contribute to the energy of the universe and in all of its vastness, no other fragment of the constellation of energy and matter bears the precise capacities that we bear. In the universe we embody a cauldron of talent unduplicated in all of the vastness that lies before us. We are not objects located in an alien world; we are subjects defined by the world's embrace.

The most intimidating connection of our personal lives is the overlap of our lives with the lives of other people. In our personal experience, two boundary conditions bear upon us most intimately. Those two boundaries are death and the inescapable presence of another person. The mystery of death is a boundary that we approach with considerable symbolism and ritual. You and I live between the "not yet" and the "no longer." And those boundaries of the "not yet" and "no longer" turn out to be powerful connections that influence and shape the in-between.

Just as awesome a boundary is the boundary condition of another person. In this case, we are connected, we interact, we are dependent upon, we partner with, we are subject to, we meet with respect or with prejudice the unfathomable presence of another person. Sheer fear causes human beings to try to connect with others through control, manipulation, and other forms of power. It is our human effort to control, to name the mystery. Yet, despite all of our efforts to manage the existence of others, we cannot gain control over their inner being. We can manage them, manipulate them, even kill them, but we cannot eradicate the singularity and the limitation they impose upon our being here.

The forces of control are actually ways of denying or trying to eclipse our interconnectedness. The relatedness of persons is the ontological predecessor to the existence of the self and the other. We are nothing without the human embrace. Fear deafens our capacity to hear the calling of the other that lies within us. Setting ourselves over against the other becomes ultimately a self-destructive act. The enduring truth is that we belong to one another and one of the most serious challenges of learning is to be able to open ourselves to the power of relating with openness and integrity. It is a process filled with risk and vulnerability, but it is the only process by which an individual can claim the meaning of being free.

Finally, the way into the essential connectedness of our lives does not lie among the vastness of the heavens or trying to find our way through the unbreachable "otherness" of the other. Author and teacher Parker Palmer points us in another direction when he tells us that "vocation does not come from a voice 'out there' calling us to become something I am not. It comes from a voice 'in here' calling me to be the person I was born to be."[1] The place to meet the "Thou" of the universe and the "Thou" of the other person is within.

The searching of our core undergraduate experience is not, after all, ultimately about the texts we study. It is about what the texts expose and illuminate about the human spirit. The texts probe difficult and enduring dilemmas and confront human conflict. Yet, in the final analysis, the text is about bringing us light and hope—the almost desperate longing for hope that lies only half-hidden behind the shroud of confidence, even arrogance, of those we teach. Our work is about enabling people, faculty and students alike, once again to become learners, to enable them and us to see and to hear the gifts with which we arrive in the world and which we spend the early years either abandoning or letting others replace with their own controlling definitions which they would like to impose upon our lives.

If I may be indulged one more citation from Parker Palmer:

> In families, schools, workplaces, and religious communities, we are trained away from true self toward images of acceptability; under social pressures like racism and sexism our original shape is deformed beyond recognition; and we ourselves driven by fear too often betray true self to gain the approval of others.[2]

I commend to you that the high purpose, or, if you will permit me, the "calling" of our teaching is to ensure that higher education does not simply provide higher training as the follow-on to lower training. There is indeed an important place for higher training in the undergraduate experience. Yet our calling lies elsewhere. It is nothing less than assuring that the human spirit is set free, that every person is set free to hear her calling,

---

[1] Parker J. Palmer, *Let Your Life Speak: Listening for the Voice of Vocation* (San Francisco: Jossey-Bass, 2000) 10.

[2] Palmer, *Let Your Life Speak*, 12.

and that every person is set free to understand the inner truth that is illuminated by the light within. Our work as educators is to be lanterns of light, helping people define the meaning of their being present in the world. Your calling and mine, our high and noble calling, is nothing less than to help young men and women find their way toward becoming more fully human and to become better citizens of the world to become free, and in their freedom become light and hope for a new generation.

CHAPTER TWO

Poetry and Professing

By Gordon Johnston
Mercer University

So what shall I do? I will pray with my spirit, but I will also pray with my mind; I will sing with the spirit, but I will also sing with my mind.

1 Corinthians 14:1(NIV)

In the essay "The Higher Calling of the Undergraduate Experience," R. Kirby Godsey defines education as "enabling every person to become a person." But what is a person? At what point can one be said to have arrived at full personhood? These questions are not simple nor easily answered. They aren't even easily asked: the professor who greets his class with claims that he is going to bring them to personhood is naturally going to stir resentment and suspicion. *Am I not a person already?* the student asks, and rightly, for he or she has usually had the sovereignty to have made some pivotal decisions, including whether to pursue a higher education. The singularity of *person* also creates a problem; for many, the word seems to refer to what we all individually are, simply by virtue of being human. In legal contexts, *person* refers to one's body. The word *self*, less unitary and empirical, suits education better. *Self* connotes an interior identity rather than an exterior one and when we talk about education, especially as a process that enables, it is the student's interior that is undergoing change. A self in our civilization, if the cliché is to be believed, has to be sought and found. Whichever word we use, I suspect we are talking about enabling everyone in the classroom to become fully alive—alive in moral, physical, spiritual, and intellectual dimensions. As Richard Hugo phrases it, we are saying to students, "You are someone and you have a right to your life. Too simple? Already covered by the Constitution? Try to find someone who teaches it. Try to find a student who knows it so well he or she doesn't need it confirmed."[1] Speaking on a human scale, we are talking about engendering by way of the classroom a consciousness in individuals that will prevent our repeating the great crimes of the past hundred years or so—among them the genocides of the Holocaust and the American west and the Balkans, slave-trading and racial segregation in the United States, apartheid in South Africa, the ethnic and internecine "cleansings" of Rwanda and the Sudan, and the terrorist attacks of 9/11 in New York and Washington and over Pennsylvania. In each of these crimes nascent persons or selves have been the tools by which murder has been perpetrated. The perpetrators of these acts had a strong sense of vocation, insofar as vocation is dutifully answering the call to work for a perceived larger good. Each of these enormous personal failures—failures of soul, of conscience, of fundamental humanity—was at its root a failure of selfhood. There can be awful totalitarian answers to the question *To what will I give my life?*

Some failures of imagination are criminal. None of these human tools had the capacity to imagine himself or herself as another person—a person of different parentage or faith. If they once had empathy, they surrendered it in the cause of misguided reverence. Their leaders turned the human sacraments of myth and symbol to depraved purposes. William Carlos Williams once said, "You can't get the news from poems, but men die miserably every day for lack of what is found there." What is found in the poem as a piece of oral or literary art is a fundamental humanity, a singular yet vatic voice speaking to whoever will listen and thereby implying that each of us is entitled to such a voice. But poetry also means that which, according to Emily Dickinson's definition, takes the top of your head off. For the teacher, poetry lies in whatever first drew him or her into committed studenthood—tree frogs, Jane Austen, string theory, the reconstruction South, etymology, the Crab nebula, the musical compositions of Charles Ives, minstrelsy. Any of these poetries is a potential answer to *To what will I give my life?* Walt Whitman says in *Song of Myself*, there is "no object soft but it makes a hub for the wheel'd

---

[1] Richard Hugo, *The Triggering Town* (New York: Norton, 1979) 65.

universe."[2] There is the pedestrian, universal gravity of Newton and then there is a more mysterious, particular gravity in which the two bodies in attraction are the subject of study and the imagination of the scholar, the artist, or the scientist—or sometimes, blessedly, an articulate amalgamation of the three, like Pattiann Rogers, Annie Dillard, or Barry Lopez. Newton's gravity holds us to the ground in a day-to-day immanence we share with everyone else. Whitman's gravity, on the other hand, is transcendent, holding us in orbit, individually isolated, centered on the subject of observation and contemplation. We're in a place that is not the absolute zero of space but that is decidedly cool. We're alone, not lonely, and we're looking. We're happy here not despite the isolation and the coolness but because of them. They grant us the office of witness. At the risk of sounding flaky, the moment of meeting our subject is like the moment the poet begins work on the poem. Stanley Kunitz describes that moment well: "You don't choose the subject of contemplation. It chooses you." We let it chasten us.

I say *chasten* because whatever our individual poetry is, science or art, it has an inexplicable authority and necessity in our lives that we try to but never quite comprehend. Traditionally, the poet has been regarded since the days of traveling bards, like the *ollamh* of Ireland (each the master of more than three hundred tales), as the keeper of important stories that have a certain chastening imbedded within them. Such stories asserted the tribe's definitions of the sacred and the profane, the person and the community, though the keeper of the tale offered only the narrative. It was each listener's task to find himself in the tale, to engage it. Interpretation and application—arriving at an ethic by which to live and participate in the community—were the listener's responsibility. The scholar, artist, and scientist have a similar relationship to their subject of study. Their discipline is a means of making the world narratable. Where those nascent selves I mentioned earlier went wrong was in abdicating their obligation to interpret for themselves. Their religious, ethnic, and nationalistic stories were interpreted for them and thus used to leverage them toward slaughter. Perhaps education isn't enough by itself to prevent

---

[2] Walt Whitman, *Song of Myself*, in the *Norton Anthology of Modern Poetry*, 2nd ed. (New York: Norton, 1988) 33.

such crimes, but I wouldn't be a teacher myself if I didn't believe it could save at least a few lives.

If the singer of tales was to an extent the voice of a culture, a preserver of stories that were revered and authoritative, he was also often a stranger himself, literally—a sort of itinerant oral anthology. In every chanting of a tale there were several implicit conversations taking place: one between a community and an other; one between the people and the past, both as depicted in the tale as history and as depicted in the audience's past hearings of the same story; another between the people and the present, the story as it is being narrated in this incarnation; and yet another between the people and the future, in the story's being handed along to the next generation. In this way the old songs—and no less many poems being written now—draw together the familiar and the strange to bring about a new vision.

The meeting of professor and students is much like the meeting between the old poet/keeper of the tales and his audience. Both professor and poet offer archetypes to an audience looking for a narrative by which to understand the world and their place or lack of a place in it. The implicit conversations that take place in the telling of the tale to an audience also take place in the classroom, which is first and foremost a place to keep touchstone knowledge. Colleges and universities identify and package essential knowledge, which makes professing a conserving activity. In the classroom the important breakthroughs of the past, the relevant work being done now, and the plateaus that we hope the discipline reaches all meet. But, like the singer of tales, the professor's primary service to the community is as conserver. No one seeks out the tale-teller for the story in progress. We want the one that is whole. There is the illusion that it is a complete package. It isn't, of course: intellectual and moral growth come by way of argument and the most urgent argument in the teacher's life takes place between this conserving, respectable professorship and poetry as defined by Dickinson—that which takes the top of the head off.

Here is a harsh truth: many of us teachers haven't earned our advanced degrees or entered the teaching field because we want to help students. It isn't Martin Buber's I-thou meeting between student and teacher—what Godsey has called "the intimate, powerful, and transforming experience of connecting"—that drives us. Instead, we connected with a Whitmanesque soft hub that gave us a cosmic wheel to decipher, and the connection was so incandescent that we had, if not to articulate it, to at least speak *about* it to someone else, even to someone to whom it would seem esoteric. For the most introverted among us and those farthest out in their orbits, the connection was such that we would do anything to stay near our precious thing, including teach. While most of us treasure I-thou meetings with pupils—we had them ourselves as students, we recognize and respect their power, and, when they occur and we are aware of it, yes, we can be transformed—we must bear in mind what brought the meeting about in the first place, the altar over which student and teacher meet. If that altar is anything but the subject we risk demagoguery, condescension, and profanity. If the only ground for the meeting is the student's need then we only extend and magnify the student's focus on his own insufficiency, his own inadequate self. Our more urgent task is to broaden the pupil's knowledge while simultaneously broadening her reverence. That means letting him or her not simply see but enter our reverence, saying *Here is the ground on which I have built an (almost) adequate self.*

I'm not speaking of evangelism. The teacher doesn't identify truth so much as show students how others have found it and what the tools of the search and their proper uses are. The most important lesson isn't *Here is the truth*. It is *The truth must be found.* Students witnessing their teachers' immersion in the subject, aside from learning from them, are witnessing a powerful, meaningful connecting. If they don't themselves orbit the subject as the teacher does they at least learn that there are things worthy of such long contemplation; they see more and are likely to find their own proper orbits sooner. Those of us most at ease among people find teaching a natural extension of our witnessing of the subject; teaching is to a large degree explaining and, often, if you can't explain something you haven't mastered it. Moreover, real mastery is impossible unless the potential master retains something of what Buddhists call the beginner's mind. It impels the search for metaphors, analogies, and figures to explain and clarify the subject—figures that can lead to new ways of seeing or pursuing knowledge about the subject. The point I'm coming to is that, ideally, teaching serves the subject. As Donald Phillip Verene puts it in *The Art of Humane Education*: "Only some of those with degrees and positions in philosophy are philosophers, only some with degrees in history really have a fundamental, historical sense of things, and only some with degrees in literature are truly literary. There are always more bodies, so to speak, than there are souls."3 The teacher's task is to be a soul. In that way she will meet, in the fullest sense of the word, both the student and the subject. The student often assumes that she is a person because other persons seem to recognize her as such as they walk down the street; professors who are "souls" to their disciplines belie this assumption and present a slightly strange but still transcendent alternative to the immanent "street soul." Often the magnetism is reciprocal: the scholar, artist, and scientist are each held to the habit of reentering the community by the act of teaching, regularly descending from their cool zeroing around the subject to engage others in conversation about it and, as far as they are able, explain its relevance to the grounded.

I admit I'm describing a teacher-student relationship fraught with potential misapprehensions and missed connections. It's often unsatisfying to both parties, but it is better than the current trends in college teaching. As Verene defines it in *The Art of Humane Education*, "Modern teaching is classroom management and career management, an extension of administrative aims to the learning process. Students exit the university having learned the art of taking courses and developing a resume of their years as a student. What has been learned is not so much chemistry, or history, or philosophy as a corporate sense of life, how to pass a course, how to participate. How to think or how to read, if learned, are fringe benefits, for what has most been learned is how to graduate."4 No self-respecting teacher wants any part of teaching people how to graduate. Rather, my role, directly as a teacher and indirectly as a writer, is to become the agent for whatever change must come about in the student to enable him or her to engage all three of the dimensions of the inner life—intellectual, moral, and spiritual. Thomas Merton implicitly defines such a student, and defines the self, in *The New Man*:

> For a man to be alive he must exercise not only the acts that belong to vegetative and animal life, he must not only subsist, grow, be sentient, not

---

3 Donald Phillip Verene, *The Art of Humane Education* (Ithaca: Cornell University Press, 2002) 22.
4 Verene, *The Art of Humane Education*, xii-xiii.

only move himself around, feed himself, and the rest. He must carry on the activities proper to his own specifically human kind of life. He must, that is to say, think intelligently. And above all he must direct his actions by free decisions, made in the light of his own thinking. These decisions, moreover, must tend to his own intellectual and moral and spiritual growth. They must tend to make him more aware of his capacities for knowledge and for free action. They must expand and extend his power to love others, and to dedicate himself to their good: for it is in this that he finds his own fulfillment.[5]

From this course of study there is no graduation, because there is always another, fuller knowledge at which to arrive—and another, fuller selfhood as well. In order for students to start down the path toward teaching themselves and making what Merton calls free decisions, they must grow a sort of mental opposable thumb—an organ of thought that enables an individual to have important interior arguments. I'm calling it a thumb because the thumb's ability to collide with the other fingers of the hand is the key to its grasp, and mental and imaginative grasp depend on similar collisions and oppositional tensions in the mind. As Verene phrases it, "Wisdom is dialectical speech that combines and moves in terms of opposites, the ultimate opposites being the divine and the human."[6] Wisdom is not simple to teach. It is often difficult enough to make me worry that for many students I'm the wrong teacher. All of the great teachers on whom I have modeled myself have been elementally articulate, but never in intellectual, moral, *and* spiritual spheres. While it is possible in life to be many things at once, it is hard to say everything at once. We think of teaching as saying, but it is also being, and often being is the more important of the two. Being what? Many things at once—in my case father, artist, student, believer, and spouse—but especially a soul. Ideally, teaching is bringing students to preparation not for careers but for the endless dialectics of their lives. None of the perpetrators of the crimes I mentioned earlier had such mental opposability either of conscience or intellect—and all of them fatally conflated the divine with the human, which allowed them to be criminally mistaught.

---

[5] Thomas Merton, *The New Man* (New York: Farrar, Straus, and Giroux, 1961) 7.

[6] Verene, *The Art of Humane Education*, 3.

I said above that teaching is centered first on the subject. Its second priority is a kind of meeting, though not exactly the interpersonal meeting identified by Buber's idea that all real living is meeting. Most of us have engaged in Buber's sort of meeting by our mid-adolescence (granted, often with a teacher). While we may not have been entirely successful in these early meetings, we at least know that this kind of relationship exists, and we will, to the degree to which we need it, seek it out. So the second priority for the teacher is not meeting the person of the student but meeting the larger world—that world that is the context for our subject of study. We must, for example, "meet" the hummingbird in its hyper, pugnacious life, and the black hole in the Perseus cluster that has been sounding a B-flat note 57 octaves lower than our ears can hear for 350 million years. If we don't we run the risk of assuming that only the human is worth meeting. We find in these nonhuman meetings our own humanity—a propensity for admiring, even loving, that which is utterly unlike us. This is the grace of our work and it is essential in the classroom. While our disciplines do often absorb us and minimize our attention to our own interiors, they also mysteriously deepen those interiors in ways we understand but struggle to articulate. For many teachers that is always going to be where the student comes in—as the auditor, the audience, the person who makes the articulation necessary.

Before students can say anything for themselves or pursue free decisions made in the light of their own thinking, they must become self-conscious. My first experience of this self-consciousness came about in my freshman year of college when I read Plato's "Allegory of the Cave" in Sara Wingard's English class and not only became aware of the many removes that separate the individual from the "true light of day" but was forced by my professor to locate myself among those removes. Was I a prisoner chained in the pit of the cave, mistaking shadows for real things? A freed prisoner squinting in pain at the fire that made the shadows? A man in the outside air looking up at the sun? For the first time I found myself thinking about myself thinking—and I repeatedly identified with the prisoner who, on being brought from deep shadow to roaring fireside, turns away at first from the painful light. The battle between the natural physical reflex of shutting the eyes to light and the intellectual and spiritual compulsion to comprehend that same light became my image for opposability. My junior year of college Dr. Wingard assigned me the reading of John Henry Cardinal Newman's *The Idea of a University*, in which I underlined these sentences: "Education... gives a man a clear, conscious view of his own opinions and judgments, a truth in developing them, an eloquence in expressing them, and a force in urging them. It teaches him to see things as they are, to go right to the point, to disentangle a skein of thought, to detect what is sophistical, and to discard what is irrelevant."[7] I have been disentangling skeins of thought ever since, and arriving again and again at a renewed sense of who I am. I couldn't become a self until I had a conscious view of my own opinions and judgments and an awareness that they were often formulated or acculturated into me without my choosing to embrace them. Once I became conscious of my own limitations in intellect, sympathy, and experience, chiefly by reading and rereading widely, I began (and continue) to try to transcend those limitations, which in turn led to my developing "just" opinions and judgments rather than unduly prejudiced ones. In my own experience with students I find that they, too, often need Newman's conscious view before they can embark on the journey to selfhood. While they need to see things as they are in the empirical world, their more urgent need is to see them as they are in their own minds, colored by countless subtle human prejudices. Then they can go about identifying and eliminating the sophistical and the irrelevant, which they will continue to do for the rest of their lives.

There are difficulties in Newman's definition of education. The challenging words are *truth* (which in this age of relativism makes those committed to accuracy squirm) and *sophistical* (which connotes deliberate, possibly devilish deception) and the phrase *teach him to see things as they are* (again for reasons of relativism—the teacher can only teach things as he sees them and, given the nature of language, what is taught is likely to be at least partly misapprehended by the student). They make me uncomfortable, too, because they call on me at least to try and follow, with my students in tow, the intellectual minutiae of my field into a broader universe where humanity and morality wait to be spoken to—where

---

[7] John Henry Newman, *The Idea of a University* in the *Norton Anthology of English Literature*, Vol. 2, ed. M.H. Abrams (New York: Norton) 1237.

sophistry has to be identified. Graduate study hasn't prepared me for this—has, in fact, encouraged me to put knowledge between myself and vital dimensions of my inner life. "If I had to limit myself to one criticism of academics, it would be this," Hugo writes in *The Triggering Town*. "They distrust their responses. They feel that if a response can't be defended intellectually, it lacks validity."[8] This tendency is understandable, especially among teachers in the liberal arts, where either the expansive self-consciousness I spoke of earlier or what is left of the scientific method always threatens to close out the conscience and the imagination. Pattiann Rogers's poems often begin in this gap where art and science fail to push through to ultimate human questions that may also have divine implications. Witness one such question from *The Dream of the Marsh Wren*: "What does it mean to the heart, to a sense of justice, for example, to realize that the earth, once begun on its quick spinning, immediately began to slow, the sun to die, the moon to move away? In light of these facts, what does it mean to act honorably? How is the definition of integrity, of hope affected?"[9]

Good teachers bring their students and themselves around to an enlarged self-awareness, but even the best teachers struggle to articulate the obligations that come with that awareness. Merton in *The Wisdom of the Desert* offers strong words to fall back on. For him, love takes primacy over everything else, including knowledge, gnosis, asceticism, contemplation, solitude, and prayer: "Love in fact *is* the spiritual life and without it all the other exercises of the spirit, however lofty, are emptied of content and become mere illusions."[10] Merton goes on to describe a love that is especially appropriate to the kind of teacher I have been describing in this essay: "Love takes one's neighbor as one's other self, and loves him with all the immense humility and discretion and reserve and reverence without which no one can presume to enter the sanctuary of another's subjectivity. From such love all authoritarian brutality, all exploitation,

---

[8]Hugo, *The Triggering Town*, 62.
[9]Pattiann Rogers, *The Dream of the Marsh Wren* (Minneapolis: Milkweed Editions, 1999) 60.
[10] Thomas Merton, *The Wisdom of the Desert* (New York: New Directions, 1977) 17.

domineering, and condescension must necessarily be absent."[11]

In my experience Buber's I-thou conversation between professor and student must be predicated on an older and continuing I-thou exchange inside the teacher that, since I'm a writer and teacher of poetry, I will describe by way of poetry. In his book *A Difficult Grace*, Michael Ryan emphasizes Emily Dickinson's immersion in traditional Protestant Christianity. Dickinson, he estimates, had heard 1,500 sermons by the time she was twenty-one. By way of comparison, a person of the same age today has heard and seen at least as many commercials on television. Dickinson, however, despite this immersion found her way through art to an original spirituality that took on ambiguities head-on—that in fact articulated ambiguities that the last four generations of American poets have continued to explore in new and revealing ways. Her poems by turn are filled with spontaneous, ecstatic vision and the most modern and skeptical relativism. In one poem, she sings about death and immortality to the tune of "Amazing Grace;" in another the brain is "just the weight of God."[12] Her body of work may be the most influential overheard conversation in American literature; the turns and counter-turns between them, their zig and zag between ecstatic vision and earthbound fatality, are themselves an I-thou conversation in the Martin Buber sense. The poet—and you can substitute *person* or *self* for poet in this sentence, the person or self upon whom education acts—is a stranger to herself in the act of writing the poem. If she is more than a hack who insists on writing what she already knows, on crafting something predetermined, the poet will be taken by her work into strange places where what she knows already is nothing next to what she might come to know, to what the poem knows. In the articulation of the poem, in the perfection of the words and the silences in the poem, in their right configuration into endlessly suggestive constellations, the artist discovers what she knows. To borrow from Hugo, she writes through whatever triggered the poem to the poem's true subject.

If you can know something somewhere in yourself and yet not know

---

[11]Merton, *Wisdom*, 18.

[12]Emily Dickinson, "712" and "632" in the *Norton Anthology of Modern Poetry*, 2nd ed. (New York: Norton, 1988) 52, 51.

that you know it, then you can be a stranger to yourself, no matter how self-conscious you are. By making the familiar strange the poet brings the listener or reader to see the world as it is (or as the poet would have it be) rather than as the reader expects it to be. At the very least the listener has seen through someone else's eyes and arrives, if not at empathy, at least at a thoroughly broadened consciousness. If the familiar can be made strange, strangeness itself ends, and the stranger or other who was once so easily demonized becomes a familiar. The office of the poem, Williams's "thing that is found there," is the foundation of that empathy that the failed selves I mentioned earlier lack—the lack that destroys their humanity as absolutely as it murders their victims. In the case of each of the crimes mentioned earlier, murder could only be carried out if the planners of those murders could subvert empathy, self-consciousness, and personal, contemplative interpretation in their followers. This subversion is not hard to accomplish if the followers are hungry and hurt, are denied meaningful and productive work, and if they come out of a tradition that reveres certain narratives. One must simply turn the narrative to his or her purposes by means of interpretation. In other words, the demagogue uses all the other offices of symbol and myth as they have always been used, but reserves to himself the right to interpret these symbols and myths and to use these interpretations as political levers. The demagogue tells people how they ought to feel.

If higher education is going to subvert this, the first relating that must be done by the teacher, the first I-thou relationship that must be begun and sustained and somehow modeled for students is the interior one. If there is a respect in which our professoriate is undereducated, it is this one. We meet no strangeness in ourselves and so we meet nothing of ourselves in the stranger who is the student, who is the ultimate, many-faced other. No one of our students can be a thou unless we have a thou inside us that we're already sporadically connecting with. I say sporadically because this thou is elusive, secretive, and always changing: our *I*'s and *thou*'s are under constant shift and revision, because there is always another, fuller personhood at which to arrive. This is why, like Louis Simpson, the committed poet's favorite poem is always the next one he writes. It may be our most important job as stewards of education to engender in students an awareness of their own thou. That is likeliest to happen when they witness their own teachers in I-thou conversation with themselves.

This brings me to my final point about Dickinson, which is also about the teaching of vocation. Ryan says that Dickinson's was a life of vocation. He sees the poems, which in her own words are her "letter to the world, that never wrote to me,"[13] as products of the most essential seeking a human being can engage in. Her distinctly lonesome vocation, begun and completed entirely in the house, yard, and village of her birth, was to answer the call she heard with her poems, which in turn become an answer (call it a meeting or a connecting) for countless others—better yet, the beginning of many answers for others. When it comes to vocation, Ryan says, Dickinson shows us not how to do it, but that it must be done. There is an important distinction here. Vocation can only be recognized by the lone self, listening. As teachers we must remember that this is the case. All we can do is model. Press very far beyond that and you may find yourself facing a student as I did last year. He was the son of a friend and after all our discussion of vocation in First-Year Seminar he came to my office to tell me that he had listened inside himself, but that there was no voice there. "I feel like some kind of ethics fool," he said. This is what happens when the thou or the self is mystified into something a little too good to be true, something that resolves the question of what a person's life is. The only final answer to this question is death. All the other answers are temporary and lead to new questions. As Rogers says, "We define, even knowing our definitions will be never ending, never secured, always changing, constantly resisting themselves, constantly determining themselves. This is our burden and this is our blessing."[14] When teaching vocation the teacher is wise to bear this in mind—and the teaching poet, which all of us are if we accept a broad definition of *poet*, is wise to hope that his poems will be articulate in ways that he as teacher cannot hope to be. "No job," Hugo writes at the very end of *The Triggering Town*, "accounts for the impulse to find and order those bits and pieces of yourself that come out only in the most unguarded moments, in the wildest, most primitive phrases we shout alone at the mirror. And no job modifies that impulse or destroys it. ... We are all going into the dark.

---

[13]Dickinson, "441" 49.

[14]Rogers, *The Dream of the Marsh Wren*, 50.

Some of us hope that before we do we have been honest enough to scream back at the fates. Or, if we never did it ourselves, that someone, derelict or poet, did it for us once in some euphonic way our inadequate capacity for love did not deny our hearing."

CHAPTER THREE

Falling Into Grace

By Charlotte Thomas
Mercer University

I really do not know what it means to fall from grace. Every time I have
fallen, I have been caught. Every time I thought that my misguided
ambitions had led me astray, I found that I was right where I belonged. We
like the idea of having control and garnering recognition for who we
become. We want to be agents in our development, and rightfully so. But,
as a very young child, I learned that not all passivity is created equal. Giving
yourself to a powerful experience—rendering yourself submissive to
it—can be ennobling and empowering. It took me decades to make sense
of what I knew on instinct as a seven year-old, but I did seem to know it
back then. I knew that I could fall into grace. Perhaps some story-telling
is in order.

I am a ninth-generation Floridian, born and raised in St. Petersburg.
That my family is Southern, despite Florida's reputation, may perhaps be
credible to you, since you now know that I know where my family was nine
generations ago. Back in Florida's territorial days, my family lived in Port
St. Joe; but for the last four generations, mine included, Pinellas County
has been home.

Unlike Port St. Joe, Pinellas County has changed a great deal in the
last hundred years. When my great-grandfather arrived around the turn of
the twentieth-century, Florida's west coast was wild, and he was a pioneer.
His father's orange grove outside of Crescent City had frozen that winter
and, in early spring, the family home place burned to the ground. All of
the thirteen children were told that they would have to make their own
way, since my great-great-grandparents could no longer support them. So,

my great-grandfather was married in a triple wedding ceremony (with one of his brothers and one of his sisters), and he headed west, west Florida, that is.

By the time my grandmother became conscious of the world around her, St. Petersburg was a lively city, but she and my grandfather chose deliberately to buy a house on the edge of town near forests and swampland. So my father grew up within ten miles of his great-grandparents' home, but he spent his days hunting and fishing, gigging frogs and catching alligators.

The St. Pete of my childhood was an over-developed, asphalt-encrusted city. It was a fine place to grow up, though. The sky was almost always blue, I never minded the heat, and there were endless opportunities socially, culturally, educationally, etc. I grew up with my grandmother and father telling me of the city they'd known, what lay behind and beneath the ground I covered every day. But my city wasn't their city, except for isolated, quickly evaporating puddles that they'd make sure I'd see. I still drive around each time I visit to try to find residue of their Florida, as an homage I suppose, but it gets much more difficult each time.

My father knew that there was little in Pinellas County that could give my sister and me a sense of what Florida had been for him as a boy, so he made a great effort to get us to more rural areas of the State. One result of his endeavors was our annual trip to Manatee Springs State Park, near Chiefland, Florida. From the time I was three years old until I was married and had to divide holidays between two large and loving families, I spent Thanksgivings at Manatee Springs.

The sharpest memories I have of Manatee Springs are of solitary moments. Even as a young child, I made opportunities for solitude on those camping trips. I would wake early in the morning, slip silently out of our campsite, walk alone to the spring boil, and sit for a while watching the quiet, powerful churning of the water through the morning mist. Tens of thousands of gallons of water per minute are pushed out of the ground at the spot. The peaceful strength of the spring awed me. And the water was impossibly clear. Although I knew from swimming in it that the boil was more than thirty feet deep, you could see details on small rocks that lay on the bottom.

Since the spring water stayed a constant 71 degrees year-round, and

November mornings were usually much cooler than that, the spring also
created a thick mist. As the sun rose and the air warmed, the mist would
begin to dissipate and appear to float down the spring run to the river, so
I would follow it on the boardwalk all the way out to the Suwannee. I rarely
stayed long at the Suwannee, but I always greeted it, inhaled it
momentarily, before I returned to our campsite. Inevitably, I would smell
breakfast and hear the quiet noise of my just-awoken family as I re-entered
our world, but I'd carry with me throughout the day the calm of the spring
just after dawn.

When I was at the spring alone in the morning, my thoughts slowed
and my mind opened. Sometimes I tried to write songs or poetry.
Sometimes I tried to burn a detailed image into my memory so that I could
draw or paint it later in the day. Whatever I did for those moments,
though, I always knew I was praying. Sometimes I would pray explicitly,
but it seemed forced and redundant. I felt like I was in the presence of
God, and I wanted him to speak to me, to tell me his will for my life, but
it never came through. I could struggle to find words to describe to myself
what I was experiencing, and sometimes I found these accounts
illuminating; but words could also distract me, and that was the last thing
I wanted.

Mother Teresa was once asked in an interview how she prayed. She
answered, "I just listen." When asked what God said to her when she was
listening, she said, " He just listens, too." That description of prayer
almost knocked me down. Although I'd never articulated it to myself
before, it was precisely what I felt at Manatee Springs. For whatever
reason, then and there I was able to listen to God. My words were just
distractions, just attempts to control the situation. And my attempts to
listen for direct words, for a message or a mission, missed the point. God's
silence and God's absence are two very different things. I first learned that
at Manatee Springs.

My reaction, aside from hack poetry, rough sketches, and bad 1-4-5
pop songs, was a compelling desire to give myself over to the power and
presence I perceived. I wanted to be transformed by my submission to
what I felt in those moments. I thought I needed to produce something,
or learn something, or be able to articulate some definite message that had
been given to me, perhaps in code; but such tangible products never

emerged. It took years for me to see that all of those desires were perversions of my experience, distractions from what I've come to see as its meaning.

As I grew older and learned a few things, I found that what I experienced at the spring was classical mysticism—the pursuit of immediate union with the divine, a desire to submit my being to Being itself. The more I learned about mysticism, the more complicated my thoughts and memories of those experiences became. One of Kierkegaard's descriptions of faith in *Either/Or* became important to my attempt to make sense of my quasi-mystical moments, especially because of the comments of a classmate of mine at St. John's College.

In my Kierkegaard class, the bulk of one discussion was devoted to our attempt to understand the idea of faith as "resting transparently in the arms of the creator." Given what you now know about my Manatee Springs mornings, you can imagine that I was quite happy with Kierkegaard's account. But, Tom Donahue, a fiftyish middle-school teacher and former welter-weight Golden Gloves champion, did not share my enthusiasm. He was incredulous. "Why would anyone want to rest transparently in the arms of the creator?" he asked. "Transparency? The abdication of individuality, accomplishment, personality? Who could possibly see that as something to be desired?" "But, you would be with God," we tried to explain to him. "No," he said, "YOU wouldn't be with anyone. You wouldn't be any-where. You would be gone, transparent."

Would giving myself over to the power and grace that I experienced those mornings at Manatee Springs mean losing myself? Not just making a sacrifice, or reorienting my priorities, or accepting a mission; but really losing myself? Some part of me knew that Tom was on to something. I had never been able to give myself to those experiences as much as I wanted to, although I had tried diligently over the years. When I sat silently at the spring, I felt an overwhelming longing for the transcendent and, when I walked away, the longing remained. Perhaps if I ever were to succeed in making the connection that called me in those moments, I would be lost. I didn't know.

Reading Kierkegaard that summer at St. John's was my first indication that my experience at the Spring as a child was not unique, but was, instead, an expression of my humanity. As I read more, I learned of a tradition populated by men and women who, in myriad circumstances, found themselves in the presence of silent and silencing power. Kant's account of the sublime, Nietzsche's stories of the abyss, the prophetic literature of the Christian Bible, Heidegger's account of the clearing and his call to return to the ground of being, etc.

My adolescent response to learning that my experience was not unique was disappointment. I thought I was chosen to feel something that others could not, would not. Happily, though, I had teachers who helped me understand the wonder of connecting my most personal thoughts with the ideas of other thoughtful people. I have come to believe that overcoming the disappointment of learning that your noblest, deepest, and most beautiful thoughts are not unique is perhaps the most important and under-appreciated moment necessary for the possibility of becoming educated.

To be disappointed to learn that my moments at the spring boil were an expression of my humanity and not my particularity was just self-love, self-absorption, ego. I wanted to be unique, distinctive, the recipient of a calling all my own. But why? What intrinsic good exists in learning that I am either more sensitive, or intelligent, or lucky, or blessed than my family or my friends, or the great minds of human history? None, that I can find. On the other hand, the recognition of my consonance with humanity is an opening, the opening for the wisdom and ingenuity of all human endeavor to inform my life. I suppose that this insight sustains my commitment to teaching, as well. To show a student her humanity as it is expressed in hundreds year-old texts written on the other side of the world is to open for her the possibility of seeing her life in the light of the collective wisdom of human history.

Several years ago, I stumbled into the Basilica of St. Denis, north of Paris, and I have been enthralled by the place ever since. The first thing anyone would notice about St. Denis, or any other Gothic cathedral, is its ornate beauty. St. Denis, however, is the first of its kind. Its architect, Abbot Suger, did not copy its style from other cathedrals. Instead he created St. Denis to be a physical space to embody a theological idea. Insofar as Gothic cathedrals silence us and give us a sense of standing in the presence of God, Abbot Suger can be said to have succeeded.

Abbot Suger was enthralled by the writings of a mystic we now call

Pseudo-Dionysus, but who at the time was known as Dionysus the Areopagite, a companion of St. Paul mentioned in the Book of Acts. It was also thought that Dionysus the Areopagite was one and the same person as St. Denis, patron saint of Paris and the first Christian martyr in France. Since Suger lived and worked in the Abbey of St. Denis, reading what he thought to be the writings of the patron Saint of his abbey and his city must have been overwhelmingly powerful. And, since the story of St. Denis' martyrdom included a miracle that led to the founding of the Abbey of St. Denis, Suger might well have believed that reading Dionysus would illuminate his responsibility to the abbey, his calling.

As the story goes, Denis and two of his Christian friends decided to take the highest ground in Paris for a Christian shrine. The problem was that the hill (now called Montmartre, or "martyrs' mount") was then occupied by a pagan temple dedicated to the Roman god Mercury. So, under the cover of night, Denis and his compatriots ascended the hill, vandalized the temple, and began raising Christian images. Apparently they were so absorbed in their work that they didn't notice the Parisians coming up the hill behind them. The pagans were predictably unhappy with the three Christians and beheaded them on the spot.

One would think that Denis' story would end with his beheading, but it doesn't. After being beheaded on Montmartre, Denis rose, picked up his head, and walked north several miles. When he reached the spot where he wanted to be buried, he stopped and lay down. The icons of St. Denis unmistakably reflect this story. He's depicted as a headless figure holding his head in his hands. And, generally, his head is topped with a bishop's mitre. The spot where St. Denis finally lay down to be buried is now the site of the Basilica of St. Denis. And, if you go beneath the sanctuary and into the crypt, you will be shown an oblong hole in the dirt said to be St. Denis' grave.

When, in the twelfth century, Suger became interested in the philosophy of Dionysus, he may have believed that he was reading the writings of St. Denis, on whose miraculous burial site he lived, worked, and worshipped. There were also powerful political arguments for claiming the identity of St. Denis and Dionysus the Areopagite. A direct connection to a biblical figure would put the church in Paris on no less credible a foundation than the church in Rome.

Whether or not Suger sincerely believed that Dionysus and Denis were the same historical figure, Suger was clearly captivated by Dionysus' mystical theology. His design of the Basilica of St. Denis was an attempt to create a worldly space for Dionysian mysticism—an environment conducive to a Christian's attempt to achieve mystical union with the divine.

Although today we might think of Gothic Cathedrals as dark places, their true architectural achievement is the introduction of light into interior spaces. Ribbed vaulting and flying buttresses made large, tall windows possible. Rather than filling these window-frames with clear glass, Suger installed colorful panes in designs that depicted biblical scenes. To be in the cathedral was to be in the light of the sun, but for that light to be refracted through the stained-glass windows; just as to read the Bible was to be in the presence of God, but reflected through the biblical accounts. The beauty of God's creation and gospel was magnified and refracted through man-made beauty. And, the worshipper did not find himself outside looking in; to the contrary, once in the cathedral, the worshipper was enveloped by light and truth. Suger's cathedral was a place where God's presence would be manifest, and one's attempts to pray would be supported by a sense of seeing and being seen by God—of bathing in His silent and silencing presence.

It is no wonder that the Basilica of St. Denis has been for my adult life what Manatee Springs was for my childhood. I am drawn to these places, find solace there. I leave centered and focused. Suger designed St. Denis to be a place where one would feel what I felt as a child at the Spring. His achievement, which is inseparable from the great beauty of his church, is the inspiration of a particular human desire—the desire for transcendence. Suger hoped to cultivate this desire in order to encourage the possibility of mystical union as Pseudo-Dionysus described it. He thought that the basilica could support the human endeavor to rest, as Kierkegaard put it, transparently in the arms of the creator.

I no more achieve that mystical union with the divine in cathedrals than I ever did at the Spring. I've since come to believe, however, that such a desire is a misunderstanding of the moment. I part ways with the mystics. God's silence is not God's absence. Longing for the transcendent is not a means to an end, it is itself an end. It is in the very longing that these experiences engender in me that God's presence in the world is made manifest. It is in such longing that my finitude is clear to me, for in such moments can I apprehend, albeit without understanding, infinitude. It is I, myself, that I give to the moment; and it is I, myself, that walk away from the spring and the cathedral and into, among other places, the classroom. I recognize, now, that my awareness of the silence, my capacity to be silenced by it, is itself a moment of grace. I am given a glimpse of the power and glory of God, and I am able to see myself and my world in His light. I am thrown back into the everyday with a renewed sense of the depth and breadth of the reality in which I am immersed. So, now, I give myself to it without fear. I fall in. But I am not lost in those moments, I am found. I do not render myself useless to the world. I am strengthened by refocused perspective. I am not debased by my submission to the silencing power that silences me; instead I am inspired by it. I knew some version of this insight when I was seven years old, although I imagine I'll be reading, thinking, and teaching myself toward a greater understanding of it for the rest of my life.

CHAPTER FOUR

"Full Of Grace And Truth"
A Theology Of Teaching

By R. Alan Culpepper
Mercer University

None of us went into teaching for the money. We are drawn to teaching for various reasons, but I dare say that if you polled the faculty, the most common response would be that we love working with students, being a part of their development, and seeing them light up when they grasp a new insight. We love being the midwives at the birth of new ideas. As fulfilling as the process of teaching and learning is, I want to suggest that as teachers we are part of something even more profound. For want of a better title, I want to suggest a "theology of teaching."

I. A BIBLICAL PERSPECTIVE OF TEACHING

First, let us remind ourselves that one of God's functions in the scriptures of Israel and the church is teaching.

God as Teacher

God is remembered as a teacher in the Old Testament. The Psalmist exclaimed, "O God, from my youth you have taught me" (Ps 71:17).[1] Job marveled, "See, God is exalted in his power; who is a teacher like him?" (Job 36:22), and the prophet Isaiah promised, "All your children shall be taught by the Lord" (Isa 54:13).

As soon as God created human beings, God began to instruct them, to teach them. God blessed them, and said to them, "Be fruitful, and

---

[1] All biblical quotations in this essay are from the NRSV.

multiply, and fill the earth, and subdue it; and have dominion over the fish of the sea, and over the birds of the air, and over every living thing that moves upon the earth" (Gen 1:28). This was the first sex education! And the first ecology lesson. We still have much to learn. Notice, though, that this teaching is not something God did after creation. God started teaching on the sixth day, before God rested on the seventh day, so teaching is part of God's creative work. Human beings did not arrive on this earth fully developed, fully civilized, fully taught, finished creations. It is not too much of a stretch, therefore, to say that that part of God's creative work is still continuing.

God's teaching continued when God warned Adam and Eve about the tree of the knowledge of good and evil, when God called Abraham and his descendants into a covenant relationship and then gave Moses the Torah, which means not law but teaching, at Mount Sinai. Centuries later, the sages of Israel would speak of God's teaching activity as wisdom. The author of Proverbs wrote,

> My child, if you accept my words and treasure up my commandments within you,
> Making your ear attentive to wisdom and inclining your heart to understanding;
> If you indeed cry out for insight, and raise your voice for understanding;
> If you seek it like silver, and search for it as for hidden treasures—
> Then you will understand the fear of the Lord and find the knowledge of God.
> For the Lord gives wisdom; from his mouth come knowledge and understanding. (2:1-6)

Because wisdom comes from God, the Lord is the source of all wisdom and understanding. In other words, because God established the order of things, whatever we teach, whether it is pharmacy, nursing, education, or business, God is the source of the understanding we want our students to discover. Then, the ancient writers personified wisdom, so that Lady Wisdom could say:

> The Lord created me at the beginning of his work, the first of his acts of long ago. Ages ago I was set up, at the first, before the beginning of the earth. When there were no depths I was brought forth, when there were no springs abounding with water. Before the mountains had been shaped,

before the hills, I was brought forth.... (Prov 8:22-25)

Wisdom is found above all in the Torah, so some ancient writers suggested that the Torah given to Moses was also pre-existent and had been with God from the beginning. It was a way of saying that what God wanted the human community to become had always been part of the divine purpose.

We don't need to pile on other references to establish that teaching is fundamental to the divine purpose for humanity. It should not be surprising, therefore, that teaching became important in ancient Israel and the early church.

Teaching in Ancient Israel

For ancient Israelites, the education of one's children was a religious duty, and much of the content of what was taught in the homes was the religious tradition of Israel: "... for I have chosen him [Abraham] *that he may charge his children and his household after him to keep the way of the Lord* by doing righteousness and justice; so that the Lord may bring about for Abraham what he has promised him" (Gen 18:19). This verse underscores the importance of instruction within the family, the religious content of this instruction, its purpose (that the children might live righteously and justly), and the integral relationship of this kind of instruction to the hope of the nation ("that the Lord may bring about for Abraham what God has promised him").

At least from the time of Josiah (seventh century B.C.) the Shema (Deut 6:4-9) was the core of the religious instruction given in the home. Within the Shema is the injunction to teach it to one's children: "Hear O Israel: the Lord our God, the Lord alone. You shall love the Lord your God with all your heart, and with all your soul, and with all your might.... Recite them [these words] to your children and talk about them when you are at home and when you are away, when you lie down and when you rise." Since religious teaching given in the home was the heart of the education of Hebrew children, it was the solemn duty of every parent (Deut 11:19).

This instruction was reinforced by the celebration of the major festivals in the home and in the community. The children's participation in the preparations, excitement, and observance of the festivals created a natural context in which indelible lessons could be learned: "And when your children ask you, 'What do you mean by this observance?' you shall say, 'It is the passover sacrifice to the Lord...'" (Exod 12:26-27). Through the father's instruction in the home and his explanations of the significance of the festivals, Hebrew children were taught how God had been manifested to them in the past, how they were to live in the present, and what God's promises were regarding the future.

Hebrew children were also taught the skills they would need to be successful members of their community. Girls were taught baking (2 Sam 13:8), spinning (Exod 35:25), and all the skills required to run a household (Prov 31:10-31). Boys were taught the agricultural cycle of the year and how to work in the fields and tend sheep (1 Sam 16:11). It was common for a son to enter his father's profession (cf. the proverb in John 5:19), and the father's instruction passed on the secrets of the trade or craft.

In pre-exilic Israel, at least, the ability to write was limited to officials, priests, scribes, and the upper class. During and following the reign of Solomon the number of scribes grew and the teaching of reading and writing began to spread (1 Kgs 4:3; 2 Kgs 25:19; Jer 36:10, 12-21). Little is known about the early schools apart from what can be deduced from the writings they produced. The Book of Proverbs, for example, was probably used both for practice in writing and grammar through the dictation of its short sayings and also for instruction in its content. Schools were organized on the premise stated in Prov 22:6: "Train children in the right way, and when old, they will not stray." Teachers recited maxims orally and wrote them for students, who recited the maxims until they were committed to memory.

The importance of the period following the conquests of Alexander the Great for the development of education in post-biblical Judaism and early Christianity can hardly be overestimated. The spread of Greek culture followed Alexander. Non-Greeks learned to speak Greek and to live like the Greeks. Understandably, most Jews resisted Hellenistic culture, but knowledge of the Greek language spread quickly in Palestine and the use of double names (Aramaic and Greek, for example: Saul–Paul) became commonplace. In reaction against the spread of Hellenism, Hasidic Jews moved to make education in the Law available to a broad spectrum of Jewish young men (Jubilees 11:16; 19:14).

The origins of both the synagogue and the Jewish elementary school are obscure. The first inscriptional evidence for the existence of a synagogue comes from Schedia in Egypt and is dated in the third century B.C. Other synagogues are attested from the second century B.C. Emphasis on the study of the Torah gave the synagogues much of the character of a school. Similarly, by the first century B.C. or A.D. Jewish elementary schools originated independently of the synagogues. It was not until after A.D. 200 that the elementary school came to be firmly related to the synagogue. Rote memorization and repetition played major roles in the learning process. Study of the Law preceded its interpretation. According to rabbinic tradition (*m. Aboth* 5.21) a youth was ready for the study of the Mishnah at age ten, and at age fifteen for the study of the Talmud.[2]

Jesus as Teacher

In the gospels Jesus is called teacher 66 times (*didaskalos*: Matt 12x, Mark 12x, Luke 17x, John 8x; *rabbi/rabbouni* Matt 4x, Mark 4x, Luke 0x, John 9x), and 57 times the verb "teach" (*didaskein*) is used to describe his activity. The frequency of this title is all the more important in view of the high Christology of the gospels. Jesus called disciples, that is, students to follow him, but he taught the crowds as well. He taught in the synagogues, and in the temple, but also out in the country, by the sea, and on the mountains. In Matthew he sits (which was the customary posture of a teacher) to deliver what we call "the sermon on the mount," and the verse that introduces it says, "Then he began to speak, and taught them, saying...." (Matt 5:2). He taught from the fishermen's boat while the crowds sat on the bank of the Sea of Galilee (Mark 4:1-2), and on another occasion he taught until the crowd got hungry (Mark 6)—which on second thought may not have been that long if his students were anything like ours! He taught "as one having authority, and not as the scribes" (Mark 1:22, 27; Matt 7:29), and he delivered "a new teaching" that was new in form as well as content. He taught in parables drawn from everyday life—a topic that Jack Sammons develops in his essay in this volume. He taught

---

[2] The material on education in ancient Israel is abridged from my article on "Education" in *The International Standard Bible Encyclopedia* (rev. ed.; Grand Rapids: Wm. B. Eerdmans, 1982) 2:22-26.

a new vision of the reign of God, and his disciples said he was "full of grace and truth" (John 1:14).

Jesus also used heuristic questions effectively. The Socratic method of teaching involves posing questions and then challenging facile or traditional answers until students arrive at new insights. The Gospel of Mark illustrates that Jesus often used questions in his debates with the authorities and in his teaching of the disciples. In contrast to the Socratic use of questions, which in Plato's dialogues usually led to extended examinations of definitions, Jesus posed heuristic questions in order to lead his hearers to make an association or see the issue in a new context. At times the question is surprising and seems unrelated to the issue under discussion, but the answer to the question will shed new light on it. Note the following examples of heuristic questions:

> "Which is easier, to say to the paralytic, 'Your sins are forgiven,' or to say, 'Stand up and take up your mat and walk?'" (2:9)

> "The wedding guests cannot fast while the bridegroom is with them, can they?" (2:19)

> "Who do people say that I am?.... But, who do you say that I am?" (8:27, 29)

Posing good questions leads to further exploration and understanding, and Jesus was a master at using heuristic questions effectively. The three themes that dominated Jesus teaching were the kingdom of God, the Son of Man, and the nature of discipleship—his guiding vision, his self-understanding, and his expectations for his followers.

Jesus also acted out his parables and teachings, carrying out a demonstration in the temple, cursing a fig tree, turning water to wine, and eating with the poor and the outcast. Significantly, the Gospel of John calls Jesus mighty works "signs." In this context, a sign is an act that points beyond itself, that calls the hearer or reader to grasp the reality to which the sign points. David T. Hanson in *The Call to Teach* points out that "the Old English root of teaching, *taecan* means to show, to instruct, or, in more literal terms, to provide signs and outward expressions of something one knows."[3] Both the words and the deeds of Jesus, therefore, should be

---

[3] David T. Hanson, *The Call to Teach* (New York: Teachers College Press, 1995)

understood as his efforts to teach.

So important was teaching to Jesus' ministry that in Matthew Jesus summarized the meaning of discipleship as follows: "Go therefore and make disciples [i.e., students] of all nations, baptizing them... and teaching them to obey everything that I have commanded you" (Matt 28:19-20).[4] The ideal that everyone should be taught is clearly evident here.

Teaching in the Early Church

From Paul's letters and from Acts one sees that teaching was important in the life of the early church. The apostles taught in public (Acts 4:18; 5:21, 25) and in private (Acts 2:42). Paul used technical terms for receiving and handing on oral tradition (1 Cor 11:2, 23; 15:3; 2 Thess 2:15; 3:6), and teaching was an essential part of his work (1 Cor 4:17; Col 2:7; Rom 6:17; 16:17; 2 Thess 2:15). Another dimension of teaching in the early church may be seen in its instruction of recent converts in the basic Christian doctrines. The office of teacher probably developed in the early churches largely in response to the need to instruct recent converts (1 Cor 12:28-29; Acts 13:1; Heb 5:12; Eph 4:11; 1 Tim 2:7; 2 Tim 1:11, 4:3; Jas 3:1). This catechetical instruction appears to have included instruction in the Old Testament and Jesus' teachings, the Church, the Christian life, and traditional ethical teachings drawn from Judaism and the Greek philosophies (e.g., Jas 1:27; 3:3-6; Phil 4:8; Gal 5:22-23). These hortatory and ethical materials were used by Christian teachers in much the same way they had been used in the instruction of converts to a philosophy or to Judaism: to guide the convert along the path of prudence, wisdom, and righteousness. The apostle Paul reflected this objective when he addressed the Galatian Christians as "my little children, for whom I am again in the pain of childbirth until Christ is formed in you" (Gal 4:19; cf. Eph 4:13-14).[5]

If we are frustrated with jumping through the hoops of assessment,

---

1.

[4] I have treated the subject of Jesus as teacher at greater length in the article on education, cited in the previous note (*ISBE* 2:26) and in *The Johannine School* (SBLDS 26; Missoula: Scholars Press, 1975) esp. 220-32.

[5] For further discussion of education in the early church, see "Education," *ISBE*, 2:26-27, and *The Johannine School*, 232-46.

we can be glad we are not the apostle Paul attempting to demonstrate to some accrediting agency that he is achieving the appropriate learning outcome! Nevertheless, his contention that the purpose of education is more than just the transmission of tradition, or a body of knowledge, is one that all of us should take to heart. It is an important part of what it means to be a university that affirms "religious and moral values that arise from the Judaeo-Christian understanding of the world" (Mercer University Mission Statement).

II. TEACHING AS A THEOLOGICAL ACTIVITY

Moving beyond this extended historical review, let us now see what we can draw from it. I will develop four features of teaching as a theological activity.

1. *It really does take a community.* As important as the old image of the ideal of education is and I mean the contention that the best education takes place with the teacher and the student sitting together on a log, talking–it is wrong. Education really takes a community.

We have found that teaching is related to God's creative activity and to Jesus' characteristic words and acts. Teaching therefore became an important function of the faith community both in Israel and in the early church. Israel produced books of history, psalms, proverbs, and prophecy. It fostered teaching at the royal court, schools of prophets, wisdom schools, and later schools for Jewish boys. Similarly, the early church produced writings of astounding literary quality in the gospels, acts, and epistles of the New Testament. And in later centuries the genetic code of the Jewish and Christian traditions led to the establishment of rabbinic academies, catechetical schools, monasteries, and ultimately universities.

For the importance of mentoring communities in current reflection on the purpose and ways of education, one need only look at Parker Palmer and Sharon Parks, both of whom emphasize that effective education requires communities in which students find support, affirmation, and meaning in the pursuit of learning.[6] Among the features of a mentoring

---

[6] See Parker J. Palmer, *To Know as We are Known: Education as a Spiritual Journey* (San Francisco: HarperSanFrancisco, 1993); and Sharon Daloz Parks, *Big Questions, Worthy Dreams* (San Francisco: Jossey-Bass, 2000).

community Sharon Parks lists: "a network of belonging" that reassures and encourages the development of inner dependence, "big-enough questions" to prompt conflict and stimulate the process of imagination and ongoing development, and "encounters with otherness" that raise transforming questions, and open new ways of making meaning. Parks cites Douglas Steere's insight: "God is always revising our boundaries outward."[7] A mentoring community creates "habits of mind," "norms of discourse and inclusion that invite genuine dialogue, strengthen critical thought, encourage connective-holistic awareness, and develop the contemplative mind."[8] Worthy dreams can be a product of a network of belonging and encounters with otherness. Parks defines "worthy dreams" as "an imagination of self as adult in a world that honors the potential of the young adult soul."[9] Forming worthy dreams is therefore "the critical task of young adult faith."[10] "Access to images" is also important for the formation of worthy dreams. Among the images that are vital Parks discusses "images of truth: a world of suffering and wonder," "images of transformation: hope for renewing the world," "positive images of self," "images of the other as both similar and unique," and "images of interrelatedness and wholeness: institutions that work." Finally, Parks contends that mentoring communities are communities of imagination *and practice*, where humanizing practices are a way of life. Obviously Parks's work is richly provocative, and we can learn much from a more sustained engagement with *Big Questions, Worthy Dreams*. We would linger, but we must move on.

2. *Every course is about more than the subject matter.* In this vein, the role of the teacher includes the perpetuation of a tradition and the formation of character. The purpose of education was never merely to provide skilled labor in order to meet the economic and developmental needs of a society.[11] On the contrary, the function of education in a biblical

---

[7] Parks, *Big Questions, Worthy Dreams*, 139, citing Douglas Steere, *Dimensions of Prayer* (General Board of Global Ministries, United Methodist Church, 1982).

[8] Parks, *Big Questions, Worthy Dreams*, 142.

[9] Parks, *Big Questions, Worthy Dreams*, 146.

[10] Parks, *Big Questions, Worthy Dreams*, 146.

[11] See the critique of this utilitarian view of education in John Martin Rich, *Education and Human Values* (Reading, Mass.: Addison-Wesley Publishing

perspective is much closer to the view of the purpose of a university as it was articulated by John Henry Newman in the nineteenth century:

> This process of training, by which the intellect, instead of being formed or sacrificed to some particular or accidental purpose, some specific trade or profession, or study or science, is disciplined for its own sake, for the perception of its own proper object, for its own highest culture, is called Liberal Education; . . . and to set for the right standard, and to train according to it, and to help forward all students towards it according to their various capacities, this I conceive to be *the business of a University*.[12]

Newman's view of "the business of a university" can be traced directly to the ancient Greek ideal of *paideia*, or the nurture of the student so that each student may attain his or her highest potential.[13] Teachers are properly mentors in this process, and their role includes the following critical elements:

A. *Awakening*. Parks notes that all human beings need to be seen or noticed, and you can learn a lot about a person's pilgrimage by asking, "Who recognized you?"[14] Jesus recognized Nathanael. When Philip brought Nathanael to Jesus, Jesus exclaimed, "Behold, an Israelite in whom there is no guile." Amazed, Nathanael answered, "How do you know me?" To which Jesus responded, "I saw you while you were still under the fig tree, before Philip called you" (John 1:48 NIV).

B. *Calling*. All of us need to find our calling in life, that pursuit that is personally fulfilling while contributing to the needs of others and the betterment of society. We find that calling through discovering our own gifts and through responding to the needs we see around us. Teachers can affirm the gifts and abilities they see in students, and challenge students to see that they can indeed make a difference in the lives of others.

Company, 1968) 5-6.

[12] John Henry Newman, *The Idea of a University*, I. vii. 1; quoted and discussed by Jaroslav Pelikan, *The Idea of the University: A Reexamination* (New Haven: Yale University Press, 1992) 71.

[13] See M. L. Clarke, *Higher Education in the Ancient World* (Albuquerque: University of New Mexico Press, 1971); H. I. Marrou, *A History of Education in Antiquity*, trans. George Lamb (New York: Sheed and Ward, Inc., 1956); Werner Jaeger, *Paideia: The Ideals of Greek Culture*, trans. Gilbert Highet (3 vols; New York: Oxford University Press, 1939-44).

[14] Parks, *Big Questions, Worthy Dreams*, 128.

Jesus called disciples both to be with him and to be sent out (Mark 3:14), and after they had been with him for a while he sent them out by twos so that they could begin to practice the things he had taught them.

C. *Encouraging*. We all respond better to affirmation and encouragement than to other forms of motivation or discipline. Barnabas was remembered as the "son of encouragement" in the early church (Acts 4:36). He could not stop the famine in Judea, but he had a field that he could sell, giving the proceeds so that the church could buy food. When others would not give Paul, the converted persecutor, a chance, Barnabas stood up for him; and later when Paul himself refused to give John Mark a second chance, Barnabas stood by John Mark, who according to tradition went on to write the first gospel. Barnabas did not become the great apostle to the Gentiles that Paul was, nor did he write a gospel, but who knows whether Paul or Mark would have achieved their greatness without him?

D. *Modeling*. The distinctive mark of Jesus' teaching is that it was incarnational, that is he embodied, modeled, and lived out what he taught. He not only taught about God's grace for all; he ate with the outcasts and stayed with a tax collector. He featured a "good Samaritan" in one of his parables, and he asked for a drink from a Samaritan woman's jug.

3. *Teaching is about helping students to write their future stories.*[15] Theologically, it is important that teaching is an exercise in hope. A teacher is engaged in shaping the future, and shaping a better future. We never know what influence we may have on our students, where they will go in life, or what great things they may do. But teaching arises out of the conviction that what we say and do does make a difference, and can have a life-changing influence on our students. A teacher always believes that students can and will be more than they are now. Teaching is therefore oriented toward the future, toward providing the motivation, vision, incentive, habits, creativity, imagination, moral integrity, and resources to become something the student is not yet. Does this sound like the definition of faith in Hebrews 11:1 "Now faith is the assurance of things hoped for, the conviction of things not seen"?

---

[15] For this insight I am indebted to Andrew D. Lester, *Hope in Pastoral Care and Counseling* (Louisville: Westminster John Knox, 1995).

David Hanson challenges teachers:

> Perhaps the hardest lesson of all... is to learn to teach *as if* students might undergo change at any moment. I call this the hardest task because it encompasses change the teacher may never actually see and may never even hear about.... Teaching is an uncertain enough endeavor without having to add the burden of accepting the fact that one may never know if one has made a genuine difference .... Henry Adams wrote that "a teacher affects eternity. He can never tell where his influence stops."[16]

Permit me a personal reflection. I love to read. I can't imagine going through life without enjoying novels, history, and biographies. But then, I grew up in a home filled with books. You would have thought my parents believed that a house was not properly furnished unless it had at least 3,000 books! But that was not my father's childhood experience because his father had only an eighth-grade education. Dad had a high school teacher (Nannie May Roney) who, as he said, "gave me the gift of enjoying and appreciating reading, one of the most indispensable gifts anyone can receive."[17] That high school English teacher in Pine Bluff, Arkansas, could hardly have imagined the extent of her influence when she awaked a love of reading in one of her students seventy-five years ago! My children are still reaping rewards from her teaching.

4. *Every student is important.* Deeply rooted in Judaism and Christianity is the commitment to the infinite value of the human soul, the belief that every person is a unique and beloved child of God. The story of John A. Broadus should be repeated as an example for every teacher. Broadus wrote a classic textbook on preaching, *A Treatise on the Preparation and Delivery of Sermons* (1870), that is still in print over a century after its publication. The manuscript was a compilation of his lectures for his first preaching class, for which he had only one student–and he was blind.

---

[16] Hanson, *The Call to Teach*, 35, quoting Henry Adams, *The Education of Henry Adams* (Boston: Houghton Mifflin, 1918) 300.

[17] R. Alan Culpepper, *Eternity as a Sunrise: The Life of Hugo H. Culpepper* (Macon: Mercer University Press, 2002) 8.

III. A CHALLENGE FROM AN ANCIENT FABLE

How do we become a teacher who embodies and practices a theology of teaching? According to Tolstoy's retelling of an ancient fable in his story, "The Three Questions," a king set out to find the answer to three questions he believed held the key to success in whatever he might undertake: (1) What are the most important things one can do in life? (2) When is the right time to do them? And, (3) Who are the right people to work with in these pursuits? Sages from far and wide came to offer answers and seek the reward he promised to any who could answer his three questions, but their answers conflicted and did not satisfy him. In desperation, he disguised himself as a peasant and ventured into the woods to seek the counsel of a wise old hermit. The frail, old hermit was digging in his garden. Seeing that he was not up to such hard labor, the king took over the digging and worked until the sun was setting.

Suddenly, a man injured with a stab wound, staggered out of the forest. The king tended his wound and settled him in the hermit's hut. The next morning, the man confessed that he had followed the king into the woods with the intent to kill him because of some harm the king's men had done to his family years before. When he ran into the king's soldiers, they wounded him before he could get away from them. Won over by the king's care for him, he begged for the king's forgiveness and received his blessing.

As he prepared to leave, the king asked the hermit his three questions. The hermit responded,

> You have already answered them. Had you not taken pity on my weakness yesterday and dug these beds for me, instead of turning back alone, that fellow would have assaulted you, and you would have regretted not staying with me. Therefore the most important time was when you were digging the beds; I was the most important man; and the most important pursuit was to do good to me. And later when the man came running to us, the most important time was when you were taking care of him, for if you had not bound up his wound, he would have died without having made peace with you; therefore he was the most important man, and what you did for him was the most important deed. Remember then: there is only one important time—*Now*. And it is important because it is the only time we have dominion over ourselves; and the most important man is *he with whom you are*, for no one can know whether or not he will ever have dealings with any

other man, and the most important pursuit is *to do good to him*, since it is for that purpose alone that man was sent into this life.[18]

Perhaps, if we can become this kind of teacher, our students too will look back and say that their teachers were "full of grace and truth" (John 1:14).

---

[18] Hanson, *The Call to Teach*, 149, quoting A. Dunningan, trans., *Fables and Fairy Tales by Leo Tolstoy* (New York: New American Library of World Literature, 1962) 87-88.

CHAPTER FIVE

Parables and Pedagogy

By Jack L. Sammons
Mercer University

In the preceding essay in this anthology, Alan Culpepper noted that teaching was so important to Jesus' ministry that he could summarize the meaning of discipleship in the Great Commission as: "Go into all the world and make disciples [*i.e.*, students] of all nations ... and teach them to observe all that I have commanded you."[1] I bet something peculiar is going on in the use of the verb "command" there. For, given the primary examples we have of Christ's teaching, rarely could these be described as giving "commands." In fact, the passage from Matthew would fit better, on a reading this essay will suggest, if it stopped at the words "to observe" and used "observe" in its more typical current meaning of "to notice." The passage would then read something like "go into all the world and make students of all nations and teach them to observe." This is more fitting, I believe, because what the disciples learned to do from Christ, the lessons, that is, they would be taking with them as teachers sent out into the world, they learned primarily through his teaching them how to observe that world. The paradigmatic pedagogical method he used to do this, of course, was teaching through parables.

I would like here to examine the pedagogy of teaching through parables to see what we might learn about good teaching from it. I offer as a justification for doing this something that I think could be acceptable to any teacher: parables, despite the to-be-expected complaints by the teacher that his students did not seem to hear him and pleas by those same

---

[1] R. Culpepper, "Full of Grace and Truth: A Theology of Teaching," p. 38 above.

students for further explanations, seem to have been an extraordinarily effective teaching method by almost any measure we might apply.

Before we can begin this examination, however, we need to get some agreement on what we mean by "parable."[2] Borrowing from several sources, primarily Paul Ricoeur,[3] I offer the following definition, one obviously conceived with present purposes in mind: A parable is an extended metaphor in narrative form operating pedagogically primarily by orienting, disorienting, and then reorienting the listener to matters drawn from common life such that he or she can come to view these matters in a way that is radically different from the one with which he or she began.[4]

---

[2] There are many definitions of the word "parable" all of which are contested. There are, however, certain biblical passages about which there seems to be little quarrel. It is these passages that I have in mind here. In learning about parables I have been guided primarily by Arland J. Hultgren, *The Parables of Jesus: A Commentary* (Grand Rapids: Wm. B. Eerdmans, 2002) (hereinafter Hultgren); John R. Donahue, S.J., *The Gospel in Parable* (Minneapolis: Augsburg Fortress, 1988) (hereinafter Donahue); Sallie McFague, *Speaking in Parables: A Study in Metaphor and Theology* (Philadelphia: Fortress Press, 1975), and an excellent introduction to academic research on parables, David B. Gowler, *What Are They Saying About The Parables?* (Mahway, NJ: Paulist Press, 2000) (hereinafter Gowler).

[3] For a good summary on various attempts to define "parable" including Ricoeur's, see Donahue, *supra* note 2 at 1-27. See also, Paul Ricoeur, *Semeia 4: Biblical Hermeneutics* (Atlanta: Society of Biblical Literature, 1975) (hereinafter Ricoeur) and Paul Ricoeur, *The Rule of Metaphor*, trans. by Robert Czerny (New York: Routledge Publishing, 1977). Probably the best-known attempt, one with which I hope to be at least consistent (although narrower), is C.H. Dodd's. Dodd offered the following: "At its simplest the parable is a metaphor or simile drawn from nature or common life, arresting the hearer by its vividness or strangeness, and leaving the mind in sufficient doubt about its precise application to tease it into active thought." C.H. Dodd, *The Parables of the Kingdom*, (New York: Harper Collins, 1935), 16.

[4] There are non-narrative biblical passages, primarily similitudes, sometimes described as parables. I intend by this definition to exclude these, although Dodd did not. By defining parables in part by their function upon their audience, I also join Robert Funk's claim that only extended metaphors can be considered parables. Thus, "the meaning of a parable is inherent in its metaphorical structure and unfolding images, a metaphorical process that transforms a reader." Gowler, *supra* note 2, at 21. Gowler tells us that the "theoretical underpinnings of this Parable-as-Metaphor School were provided by ... [I.A. Richards, Philip Wheelwright, Max Black, and Paul Ricooeur]. *Id.* at note 10. See, especially, I.A. Richards, *The Philosophy of Rhetoric*, 89-138 (New York: Oxford Univ. Press, 1936).

This change comes about not by the introduction of anything new to the listener, including any new explanations, but by a jolting reminder to the listener of things he or she already knows.[5] Instead of being explained, the listener's world is *re-presented*[6] to him or her for observation anew. In simpler terms, the listener is *shown* how his or her world is; not told. Thus the parable remains open-ended, polyvalent, and generative of further inquiry by the listener. It is, in fact, one form of answering a question by asking another—a better—question.

We can get some help appreciating the distinctive features of teaching through parables if we compare this method with the current use of moral dilemmas to address the same subjects as those addressed in the biblical parables.[7] With moral dilemmas the moral work done by the student's perspective or point of view[8] on the world, the one that makes the student see the moral dilemma as a moral dilemma, is characteristically assumed by the teacher and goes largely unexamined. By contrast, the parable is designed to call the student's attention to this very perspective; to make it, that is, a subject of the student's reflection. Additionally, the point of using moral dilemmas is often to show students what they do not know; the point of parables, again by contrast, is to show them what they do know. Finally, we notice that because moral dilemmas teach us what we

---

[5] All of this may seem at first to be contradictory. How can something that is ordinary be also jolting? How can something that is already known be a surprise? This is, however, the point. For essential to the operation of the parables is that the ordinary is not what you are thinking it is and, therefore, it is surprising.

[6] By "re-present" I mean to say that the student is not offered a representation of the world of the subject addressed in the parable but a presentation of it such that he or she can see it anew. The difference is important and becomes more important for our purposes here as the argument develops.

[7] For a description, discussion, and a similar analysis of the problems with using moral dilemmas, *see* Edmund Pincoffs, "Quandary Ethics," in Hauerwas & MacIntyre, Eds., *Revisions: Changing Perspectives in Moral Philosophy* (South Bend: Univ. of Notre Dame Press, 1983). See also, Edmund Pincoffs, *Quandaries and Virtues: Against Reductivism in Ethics* (Lawrence: Press of Kansas Univ., 1986).

[8] Neither "perspective" or "point of view" is the right word here but the term frequently used, "world-view," seems awkward, unwieldy and (obviously) too global. "Attitude" is worse, in that it is even more likely to be misunderstood, although it does capture something important. Because nothing seems quite right, I have decided to stick with "perspective," hoping that the reader will read more into that one word than we usually do.

do not know, they point away from our ordinary experience, and away from the personal, from which there is presumably nothing left to be learned, and toward a more theoretical consideration of the problem posed. Parables, by contrast, point toward ordinary experience, toward the personal, and away from the theoretical. In Paul Ricoeur's apt phrase, with parables the "extraordinary is within the ordinary."[9]

Now all of this needs clarification (and, as a lawyer, I need a text from which to work). So, let me use as our example the most famous of Christian parables, The Good Samaritan.

---

[9] Ricoeur, *supra* note 3 at 118. The following comments anticipate some things that will appear later in the text but it may be useful to introduce them here. There is a close relationship here between the pedagogy of the parable and the shift in thinking between the earlier and the later Wittgenstein, especially as that shift is described in James C. Edwards, *Ethics Without Philosophy: Wittgenstein and the Moral Life* (Gainesville: Univ. of S. Florida Press, 1982), (hereinafter Edwards). Wittgenstein, described for this context, can be seen as moving from the limitation of representation-as-reality to a more metaphorical understanding of the world, one that includes Ricoeur's "extraordinary." Consider:

It is this notion of a "way of looking" that makes it possible for [Wittgenstein to attach] a supernatural value... to a natural fact. To see the existence of the world as a miracle is not to see some obscure non-natural property (the property of being miraculous) there in the world; rather, it is just to see the purely natural facts available to be seen by everyone else and to look at those facts in a particular way. It is to take toward them a certain attitude. What makes the world a miracle is the self that views it; only certain of us are capable of that wondering experience. *Id.* At 92.

Wittgenstein, of course is far from being alone in this desire to see the "extraordinary in the ordinary" or in his noticing that the issue is in representation or that this implies something about the relationship between the person and the subject observed or experienced. He would not, however, see this as a mere change in attitude as some others do, for he did not feel that such a change could be described, but only experienced through a certain cleansing of our thinking.

Other than Edwards and in addition to primary sources, in my use of Wittgenstein in this essay I have relied upon Norman Malcolm, *Wittgenstein: A Religious Point of View?* (Ithaca: Cornell Univ. Press, 1994) (hereinafter Malcolm); Joachim Schulte, trans. by William Brenner and John Holy, *Wittgenstein: An Introduction* (Albany: SUNY Press, 1992); Judith Genova, *Wittgenstein: A Way of Seeing* (New York: Routledge, 1994); A.C. Grayling, *Wittgenstein* (Oxford: Oxford Univ. Press, 1996). For the reader interested in his life, the best biography, and, to my thinking, one of the best biographies, is Ray Monk, *Ludwig Wittgenstein: The Duty of Genius* (New York: Macmillan, 1990). See, also, Norman Malcolm, *Ludwig Wittgenstein: A Memoir*, 3d edn. (Oxford: Oxford Univ. Press, 1984).

And behold a certain lawyer stood up and tempted him, saying, "Teacher, what must I do to inherit eternal life?"

"What is written in the Law?" Jesus replied. "How do you read it?"

He answered: "Love the Lord your God with all your heart and with all your soul and with all your strength and with all your mind, and, `Love your neighbor as yourself.'" "You have answered correctly," Jesus replied, "Do this and you will live."

But, seeking to justify himself, he asked Jesus, "And who is my neighbor?"

In reply Jesus said: "A certain man was going down from Jerusalem to Jericho, when he fell into the hands of robbers. They stripped him of his clothes, beat him and went away, leaving him half dead. A priest happened to be going down the same road, and when he saw the man, he passed by on the other side. So too, a Levite, when he came to the place and saw him, passed by on the other side. But a Samaritan, as he traveled, came where the man was, and when he saw him, he took pity on him. He went to him and bandaged his wounds, pouring on oil and wine. Then he put the man on his own donkey, took him to an inn and took care of him. The next day he took out two days' wages and gave them to the innkeeper. 'Look after him,' he said, 'and when I return, I will reimburse you for any extra expense you may have.' Which among these three has acted as a neighbor to the man who fell into the hands of robbers?"

The expert in the law replied, "The one who had mercy on him."

Jesus told him, "Go and do likewise." (Luke 10:25-37)

We notice that this is a metaphor in extended narrative form about an ordinary experience within the context of the lawyer's world. We notice, too, that the lawyer is first oriented toward this ordinary experience—it starts unfolding as he might have expected—then disoriented by the form the parable takes. We do not experience this disorientation now as easily as when the parable was first taught. It comes about this way: The question the lawyer asked was not facetious, that is not what asking the question "to justify himself" means. It was as serious then as it is now. Ordinarily in the lawyer's world the term "neighbor" would have referred to a fellow Jew or proselyte and the obligation any Jew would have toward such a person would have been abundantly clear: love him. The problem, however, is where does one draw the line defining those toward whom one has this extraordinarily demanding obligation?

This, it seems to me, is a public or social question much more than it is a purely personal one, and, initially, the lawyer is oriented to hear the parable as a response to such a social question. His disorientation from this occurs with two rhetorical moves. The first places two accepted obligations in opposition to each other, much as we might do with a moral dilemma. For the priest passing the man by the side of the road had a clear obligation to help him—the parable is not about the existence of this obligation—so the student, upon hearing that a priest passed "by chance," would have expected to hear that help had arrived. But the priest also had an equally clear, and now opposing, obligation to avoid the "half-dead" man. By the laws of ritual purity, priests were forbidden to touch any corpse except that of a family member. So, if the "half-dead" man were, in fact, dead—something the priest in the story would not have known—he *should* have moved to the other side of the Jericho Road. The second rhetorical move is the surprising introduction of the Samaritan into the story. Following the "rule of three" of good story-telling, and the three traditional divisions among Jews, the lawyer, after hearing about the priest and the Levite, would have expected the third traveler to be an ordinary Israelite.[10] Instead, it is a Samaritan—an apostate and an object of contempt—who is offered as an exemplar, not only offering physical aid to the "half-dead" man, but also the protection and financial assistance needed to permit him to return eventually to health and to freedom.[11] As

---

[10] This reading dates back at least to Joachim Jeremias. See, Joachim Jeremias, *The Parables of Jesus*, 204 (Upper Saddle River, New Jersey: Pearson Education, 1972). See, also, Hultgren, *supra* note 2 at 98.

[11] The money given to the innkeeper would have prevented the man from becoming an indentured servant of the innkeeper as was the practice for those who could not pay their debts at the inn. Thus, the Samaritan is not just concerned with saving a dying man but with this stranger's future well-being. According to the

a further surprise, because the extent of the Samaritan's assistance is offered as an accurate measure of love to others "as [to] yourself," this shunned Samaritan, *in his person*, is the criterion of compliance with the Law.

As I said, these rhetorical moves would have been more jolting for a listener at the time than they are for us, but I don't think it takes much moral imagination to see how, with a few minor revisions in the story to bring it up to date with our own social divisions and the objects of contempt within them, we could return the jolt to it.

After the disorientation, the lawyer is then reoriented toward an answer assumed to lie within the lawyer himself, now that his world has been "re-presented" to him for fresh observation. Nothing has been explained here, but something has been shown, and it is something that the lawyer already knew! Of course, exactly what this something is not at all clear, for the implications of it are left to the lawyer's and the reader's own further inquiry, an inquiry that is likely to be terribly frustrating.

Why frustrating? Well, for one, the lawyer's question was never answered. We do not yet know who is to be placed in the social, moral, philosophical, or theological category of "neighbor" or even how this category might work. In fact, the "answer" returned to the lawyer at the end of the parable is in the form of a different question; different, that is, from the one he asked initially. The "answer" is: "Which among these three acted as a neighbor to the man who fell into the hands of robbers?" Rather than having learned who is our "neighbor," the lawyer has instead learned how to be one! Secondly, and most importantly for our purposes, on first appearances the lawyer's question seems to have been changed from a public or social question to a very insistently personal one. And, because it is, something that was important to the lawyer's asking seems to have been left behind.[12]

King James Study Bible, "two days' wages" would have been sufficient for about two months of care at the inn.

[12] This is not unique to this parable or, within the New Testament, not unique to parables. Consider in this light Christ's healing on the Sabbath, his advocacy for the adulterous woman, including the nature of the specific argument he uses in her defense, the parable of The Prodigal Son, and so forth. Far more generally, consider that the apparently impossible tension between loving your enemy and

The lawyer's question—this is not surprising for a lawyer, but expected of us—raised an implicit concern about a community. The question of who is within the category of "neighbor," and thus owed this extraordinary obligation of love, and who is outside, is a question with what appear to be inescapable practical implications for the good of any community. This is true on the issues the lawyer might have had in mind in asking the question: for example, to whom do the obligations of protection of the widow, the orphan, the lame, and the poor, and so forth, all of which are owed to "neighbors," apply? One community cannot be responsible for all those outside it and remain a functioning community.[13] (This is of course the basic issue raised by those who now complain about the loss of American jobs to illegal immigrants or to the globalization of manufacturing or to a hundred other "political" concerns including our role in international affairs.) And it is also true on the social issues raised by the parable itself. For example, the Samaritan's acts of kindness, while admirable, are not very good ways of dealing with the underlying problems of the dangerousness of passage to Jericho, or the need for medical care to travelers in distress, or, for that matter, the hardhearted financial shrewdness of innkeepers, or, finally, the moral tensions created by the ritual purity laws through which Jews remained a faithful community.

Once we start thinking this way, other things go awry as well. We can, for example, agree on the personal morality of the Samaritan's acts but be forced to reject what he did as implying a social or legal obligation for other citizens, as most communities do now, for a variety of good reasons that are also moral ones. (If we think of the jurisprudential discussion in criminal law of failures to rescue, we will see that this is true.)

Thus, our ordinary ways of thinking about these matters readily

---

protecting your own way of life is exactly what Christ insists that we reconsider.

[13] I am sure it would not have occurred to the lawyer, as it still would not occur to us, that an unlimited law of love could possibly "work," and, if not, where was one to draw the line? The possibility of considering an unlimited law of love was so unlikely, I imagine, that the lawyer assumed that Christ would understand the question as he did, as a question about a community. In order to feel this in modern terms, we can imagine asking a similar question to a political candidate about health care for the poor or even for victims of crime and then imagine that candidate responding with the parable. One would think he or she missed the point, wouldn't one?

become challenges to the personal insight of which we were reminded by the parable. But wait! How did this happen? Nothing has changed here either in the story or in the person that I am as a student of the parable. I still "know" what the parable reminded me I knew. All that has changed in this—the only reason it has suddenly become such a puzzle for me—is the perspective that I am now taking toward the story. We can see that the parable has forced me to take notice of this change, to take notice of my relationship to the subject it addressed, and to take notice of the importance of my perspective in understanding this subject. I have been asked to examine this relationship, to observe it, just as I have been asked to examine and observe the way the three travelers took notice of the half-dead man by the side of the Jericho Road.[14]

This, then, all this, is what I mean by "parable."[15]

We can notice, and for now just notice, that there is nothing about me as a student of the parable and nothing about the lawyer to whom it was addressed that would not be relevant to the inquiry it prompted.[16] *All* of

---

[14] There is further encouragement toward this reflection in this particular parable since many students, I think, would blanch at the extent of the obligation toward the man by the side of the road assumed by the Samaritan and search for a justification for not accepting such a demanding obligation as a morally or theologically required one. The ready place to look for such a justification would be in a public or social perspective on the story. Any thoughtful person, however, would notice what he had done, I think, and thus the move would be called to such a person's attention. This, I am suggesting, is what makes this a parable. As Funk put it: "The parable is not closed, so to speak, until the listener is drawn into it as a participant." Robert W. Funk, *Language, Hermeneutics, and the Word of God*, 133 (1966) as cited in Glower, *supra* note 2 at 20.

[15] I intend here only to offer this understanding of parables for an analysis of their pedagogy. There are, obviously, strong theological implications at work involving, for example, a Kingdom that, while present, is also a work in progress and one in which truth is not a criterion but an accomplishment, but those, and other similar implications, are not my point in this essay.

[16] Another way of understanding this point, following Wittgenstein, is to realize that each way of looking at an experience is inextricably involved in a form of life. The parable, by forcing me to notice the way in which I am looking at an experience, also forces me to consider the form of life in which I am located in so doing and to consider that form in relationship to the experience. We can see this rather clearly, I think, in the effect of the parable of The Good Samaritan. We can, for example, see it in the implicit guidance it offers for compliance with the "rule" to "love your neighbor as yourself." It would be possible, indeed, typical, to

who I am is implicated in this inquiry. Because it is, the parable requires a wholeness to this "all of who I am" that I would just as soon avoid, it being much simpler and even, at times, more satisfying to divide myself up in ways that permit me to make some separate sense of each part.[17]

The challenge the parable poses for me has become a question about me—of my own complexity if you will as much as about the world it re-presented to me. But, while suddenly this is about me, the parable has not left me free to recreate this re-presented world into something more suitable for my own perspective. Instead, the world the parable re-presented to me now has an authority over me. For I saw in this world things I already knew to be true about the subject the parable addressed and cannot now deny in good faith. The parable itself, then, has the authority over me of a constraint. It seems to be one that, while not of my own choice or of my own making, nevertheless arises from my own personal relationship to this subject within this re-presented world. Like the half-dead man at the end of the parable, I am left in my inquiry with the distressing insecurity of the freedom once again to go down a treacherous road. As it would be for many students, I bet this is not the method of teaching the disciples, much less the lawyer in the parable, wanted. The disciples, of course, wanted a messiah successful by their own measure and

---

treat "love" in this legal command as "if there really were an object from which I derive its description but I were unable to show it to anyone." Ludwig Wittgenstein, *Philosophical Investigations* (Oxford: Basil Blackwell, 1953), no. 374. This is likely to be the way the lawyer is accustomed to thinking about the rule such that what is being asked of Christ is to choose an appropriate interpretation of the word. Obeying a rule, however, requires a practice, and the real question of importance, as the operation of the parable makes clear, is in which practice the rule will be obeyed. "This is how it strikes me. When I obey a rule, I do not choose. I obey the rule blindly ... obeying a rule is a practice." *Id.* at 219 & 202.

[17] Another way of understanding this is to focus upon the tension in the parable as a dialogue with the lawyer, between a social perspective and a moral one. It would be easy to fall into the modern trap of considering morals only within the personal and thus avoiding this tension by neatly dividing myself. It is this division that the parable does not permit me to make. The personal morality in the parable is offered as an "answer" to the social question. I cannot now deny this or deny that what the parable revealed to me about my self, what it told me I already knew, is social. The parable then takes me directly and personally into what might be described as the constitutive tension of Christianity.

not someone through whom that measure would change. For them, the right measure was a messiah who would impose his will upon the world through acts of control, of a setting straight, of justice. The teacher they got instead was a great surprise, and, although the use of parables may have been common in Hebraic teaching, my guess is that his method of teaching was a great surprise to them as well.[18] "If," we can imagine the disciples asking, "the message is as urgent and as important as you say it is, why not give it to us straight?" For, as every student knows, there is something reassuring about being handed new knowledge by which to work out our own wills upon the world and only insecurity in the offer of something as vague as a new way of observing that world. Surely none of us would fault the disciples for seeing in this odd manner of teaching too little structure, too much freedom, too much trust of and dependence upon students, and, with gruff practicality, too few opportunities for good note taking.

Despite what I am suggesting here about its reception—the teaching evaluations surely would not have been good—this method of teaching, as I said before, seems to have been extraordinarily successful. Why? What is it about the use of parables that makes it such an effective pedagogical method? There is, I think we can see now, a lot we could cover here: the contextuality of parables, one that includes and, indeed, requires consideration of the individualized context of the student; the nature of the relationship of teacher to student and student to teacher implicit in the use of parables (and that to which the parable appeals has authority over both); the manner in which parables accept the complexity of experience while not succumbing to it; the open-endedness and persistent generative properties of parables; the interesting combination of authority and freedom that parables provide; and the effectiveness of the metaphorical function, broadly described, of "showing" or "re-presenting"

---

[18] Not everyone would agree with the statement that parables may have been common. There is an extensive literature concerning the rabbinic uniqueness of Christ's use of parables and the uniqueness of His parables. See, for discussion, Hultgren, *supra* note 2 at 5-11. It seems to me, however, that surely the disciples would have recognized the method, and this is all that is necessary to my claim in the text that the method would have been a disappointment to them and surprising as such.

rather than of explaining or representing. All these, I think, would be profitable lines of inquiry for any teacher interested in his or her craft (and not willing to have its excellences measured solely by teaching evaluations).

They are all related, of course, and it would be difficult over time to talk about any one of them without quickly encountering the others. I wish, however, in the little time and space remaining, to focus our attention upon only one aspect of the parable as a teaching method. Not only do I believe this one aspect to be terribly important for us now, but I also believe we can get good guidance from it for the teaching of almost any serious current subject. This aspect is the nature of the relationship of the student to the subject being taught called into being through the use of parables.

Just a few moments ago, after saying that the parable of The Good Samaritan forced me to notice my relationship to the subject it addressed and my own changing perspective on it, I noted as well that the inquiry prompted by this required all of who I am. It is to this aspect that I now want to call our further attention. Of course, it is possible to think that this aspect, this requirement of noticing the relationship of one's perspective to the subject, was not a product of the use of a parable but a product of the nature of the subject this one addressed. Perhaps the parable made relevant all of who I am because its subject was ethics. Surely, however, this is not the case. We all know that it is possible, indeed, common, to teach ethics as a subject in ways that do not require a relationship with any particular self. Teaching ethics, for example, as a matter of the calculation of utilities or efficiencies or as the application of the categorical imperative could readily be done without consideration of the person of the student at all, in fact, without the requirement that a student be present! No, it was not the choice of subject that produced this effect on the student. It was not the subject itself that required the student's consideration of his or her relationship to it. It was, instead, the parabolic technique of "showing" the lesson to be learned and the parabolic use of metaphor to do this. For this combination returns to the self of the student a linguistic image of his or her own fullness in the subject addressed.[19]

---

[19] The metaphor at work in the description in the text is the metaphor of a

By contrast, other ways of teaching—ways that can be captured, far too simplistically, I fear, by describing them through an opposition of "showing" to "explaining"—necessarily limit the self's role in the study and understanding of the subject by returning to the student not the complex fullness of the student's self but a removal of that self, so that the subject matter can be made simpler, more manageable, and, thus, more perspicuous.[20] (A simple example would be explaining to the lawyer in the parable, in response to his question, that a "neighbor" is anyone in need.) These other ways are not a "re-presenting" of the world to the student as a way of reminding him of what he already knows, but a "representing" of it as something that needs to be known. The only thing of any importance about the self of the student in any of this is that this self be a generic knower of things. Beyond this sole attribute, these methods, by their very nature, encourage in the student a self-forgetfulness.[21] For all that really

---

mirror of the self. In this, as in all metaphors, both sides of the comparison—sides described by I.A. Richards as the "tenor and the vehicle"—are affected by the comparison, that is to say, we understand both compared objects just a little differently from what we did before. "A metaphor ... has an element of comparison but it functions in a completely different way [from a simile] because metaphor juxtaposes two discrete and not entirely compatible elements: A is B. This juxtaposition is creative of meaning and induces a vision that cannot be conveyed by prosaic or discursive speech. The metaphor confronts us; it produces an impact upon the imagination; it is the bearer of reality." Gower, *supra* note 2 at 20, 21, (*citations omitted*). Gower is describing the work of Robert W. Funk. What I am focusing upon in the text is the way in which the metaphor, in the form of a parable, "confronts us" by suggesting that this confrontation includes a reflection of the self confronted and, thus, what the parable calls into being is a relationship between the audience and the subject addressed in the parable.

[20] We are again with Wittgenstein here, for he often observed that the ethical could not be taught. "If I needed a theory in order to explain to another the essence of the ethical, the ethical would have no value at all." Quoted in Friedrich Waismann, *Wittgenstein und der Wiener Kresis*, Ed. B. F. McGuinness (Oxford: Basil Blackwell,1967) 116-17 as trans. and cited in Edwards, supra note 9 at 98. In our terms, this means that all attempts to represent the ethical, as opposed to those that re-present it, are doomed to failure. Thus, for Wittgenstein, and, perhaps for us, it is not a question of the parable working better but of other, non-metaphoric, non-"showing," methods not "working" at all. The trick here, of course, is to realize, also with Wittgenstein, that every subject is an ethical one.

[21] This self-forgetfulness, James Edwards says, eventually and paradoxically results in a narcissistic self-enchantment. Because the self is so clearly removed

matters in these methods is whether or not the representation in the form of an explanation is accurate. It does not matter to whom it is represented. Perhaps a large reason for the effectiveness of teaching through parables, then, is that they do demand in the relationship of the student to the subject this fullness of self, a fullness that other methods of teaching discourage.[22] Perhaps, we teachers can learn from this.

It is time, now, to recap a little. Here's what we have done thus far: I suggested that teaching through parables seems to have been effective; wondered what it was about such teaching that made it so; focused upon one aspect, the relationship of the student to the subject being taught brought into being by the use of parables; briefly contrasted this aspect with other teaching methods; and then suggested that it might be this fullness of the self required by parables that makes them so pedagogically effective.

There are very simple ways of understanding the difference between the contrasting ways of teaching I have been describing, simple ways that are within the common experience of every student. You already know which teachers and which methods of teaching work for you as parables do. There is, however, something else to be said here. It is a way of seeing in this simple difference in teaching methods something very profound at

---

from the subject of its study it takes on an enormous importance that is unrelated to that subject. He described these two effects, i.e., self-forgetfulness and self-enchantment, as Cartesian tendencies that are the "defining marks of our culture." Edwards, *supra* note 9 at 166-7. This is something, I believe, that any thoughtful teacher experiences today in her students, in her self, and in the relationship of both to the subjects of study. Paraphrasing Edwards, we are all tempted to be only viewers of the world who step back to admire ourselves viewing. Id. at 167.

[22] Since this is the central point, let me offer another (and better I think) description of it:

There are no spectators in the dialogic world of parable. The action is moved out of the horizon of the person performing the action in the past and is placed within the horizon of its contemplator. Every event, every phenomenon, every thing is represented parabolically, when it comes into contact with the present through a retelling of the story, becomes part of our world-in-making; it acquires a relationship—in one form or another and in one degree or another—to the ongoing event of our current life in which we are participating. In effect, it is an encounter of two authors. —Gower, *supra* note 2 at 101, describing the work of Ivor Jones.

work, and it is to this that we now turn.

The world learned from Wittgenstein, I believe, that there are inherent limitations to our ability to represent any reality and these limitations are there in any language we might use including—very specifically including—the languages of math, science, and economics. For Wittgenstein, the problem was not that our ability to represent, given the limitations of our languages, fails to capture a reality that could otherwise be well represented. It is not, that is, that through metaphor, for example, we can better represent a reality than through other, more literal, forms of language. It was instead that the attempt to "represent" reality itself leaves out something central to any truthful understanding of it. For there is no understanding of reality to be had that is not also a reflection of the self that experiences that reality.[23]

Now the early Wittgenstein was interested primarily in what we might call our relationship to natural facts, but later he came to understand that what was of most importance in this is the corruption worked upon us in all our endeavors by our habit of viewing the world as a reality that could be known absent our relationship to it, that is, of identifying the world, including the world of human creations and human thought, with any single representation of it external to our selves. Wittgenstein wanted to shake us free from this corruption through a philosophical therapy that was, for him, clearly an ethical matter, a matter about lives well lived. I do not think I am going too far with Wittgenstein if I suggest that what he had to say to the world was also said to teachers, and its message to us offers a confirmation and a startling extenuation of what we just learned about teaching from parables. In the terms that interest us here, Wittgenstein does not just tell us why parables might be an effective teaching method but encourages us to wonder if there are any other ways of teaching effectively, if by "effective" we mean truly teaching.[24] For, I think he

---

[23] This is to say that there is no subject apart from its relationship to the viewer of it. Thus, the "reality" of the subject is in a direct encounter with it, something akin to an earlier religious sensibility toward the world that allowed that world to be understood as miraculous. See Edwards, *supra* note 9 at 200, 236.

[24] Wittgenstein, in fact, uses the method we are describing in his own writings. They are written as he believes a teacher should teach. As he says, he is not seeking "to hunt out new facts; it is rather of the essence of our investigation that . . . we

would say, we teachers have no subjects to teach apart from our students', and our own, personal relationships with these subjects and thus we capture the truth about the subjects we teach only when our teaching reflects this. And, he might add, what is of most importance in any subject being learned, whether we *teach* it in what we might now call a parabolic way or not, is being *learned* this way. This learning is there, like the weather, whether we want it to be or not. What we can do to become better at our craft is be conscious of this.

Those readers who are students may well find this insight lik as I do. Let me, however, quickly remind them of something. The p of The Good Samaritan was not a pleasant experience for the lawyer. \ he may have learned from it was not something he wanted to learn expected to learn, nor was it done with thoughtful consideration of h feelings, his needs, his thoughts on the subject, his personal style o. learning, and so forth. It was instead rather brutal, personally embarrassing, a threat to his honor as a lawyer, intentionally frustrating, and certainly unpleasant. There is, to be sure, an inherent respect for the person in this method, but it is not a respect for what that person now thinks. This the teacher is trying to change, using a form of authority over the student about which the student has no choice because it is an authority to which he is already committed.[25] The student has not been asked to look within for guidance; this is not what being in relationship to a subject means. Instead, he has been shown what is already within. The student in the parable, the lawyer, we will remember, was left to a personal inquiry for

---

want to understand something that is already in plain view. For this is what we seem in some sense not to understand."—Ludwig Wittgenstein, *Philosophical Investigations* (Oxford: Basil Blackwell, 1953), no. 89.

[25] One way of describing this is to say that the parable is authoritative for the student rather than being authoritarian as a command might be. In any case, however, these are sources of authority about which the student has little choice. "[Eta] Linemann explains that a parable is a form of communication, a dialogue between the narrator and the listener. As such, it is an urgent endeavor, because the narrator wants to do much more than just impart information. The teller of a parable wants to influence the other person, to win agreement. The parable is the means of overcoming any resistance the hearer might have." Gower, *supra* note 2 at 14, relying upon Eta Linemann, *Jesus of the Parables: Introduction and Exposition* (1966).

which, I am sure, he felt he had not been adequately prepared by the parable and it is an inquiry that could go badly astray. I want to be clear that what I am suggesting we can learn from this aspect of teaching through parables and from Wittgenstein is not at all at odds with any of this. Not at odds, that is, with teaching and learning being the distressing and demanding business that it is in the biblical parables.

How can I be a logician before I am a human being?[26]
L. Wittgenstein

We are coming near the end of the essay and it is time now to say more about how the teaching we have been considering is to be done. Simply noticing that it is produced by extended metaphors, like our parable, is hardly enough, nor is it enough to attribute its uncommon pedagogical potential to a fullness of the self in the relationship to a subject. For, I fear, we no longer know how an increasing number of our subjects might be related to a fullness of self, either ours or our students, or, for that matter, any self at all. Because we do not see our subjects this way, there is no opportunity or opening in which parabolic teaching could work. Through the increasing dominance of *techne* in all our subjects—a dominance we grasp at, I believe, as our students do, because, as we observed before, there is something reassuring about being handed new knowledge by which to work out our wills upon the world—we distance ourselves from our subjects with much the same effect as the distancing of earlier craftspeople from the products of their labor by industrialization. Perhaps it is not so much our students who are in need of parables, but we ourselves. Let us return then to our parable for further guidance, starting with the idea with which we began, that is, that the message of the parables, the one the disciples were to take with them into the world, is "to observe."

What the parable of The Good Samaritan called to the attention of the lawyer as primary was the simple reality of the plight of the half-dead man by the side of the road. In doing so, it brought to his attention the

---

[26] The quotation is from a letter to Bertrand Russell translated by B. F. McGuinness and quoted by Peter Winch in "Discussion of Malcolm Essay" in Malcolm, *supra* note 9 at 124.

mysterious value each of us has to the other, to "soul" if your language is
that of the church, because there is nothing else about the half-dead man
to prompt our reaction to his pain; no reason, that is, that would
distinguish him from any other sentient creature. There is, with
Wittgenstein, no explanation we could give (including the explanation of
an analogy to ourselves) for our reaction to his suffering.[27] There is no way
to ground it in anything other than its personal reality to us. It simply is,
as is, for example, the trust a young child gives to her father, for which
she, too, can offer no explanation.[28] The parable said to the lawyer and says
to us: Start thinking about 'neighbor' here in this recognition of the mys-
teriousness of each of us to the other that, in candor to yourself, you must
acknowledge; not in concepts (that he has a soul; that he suffers as I do;
that all humans merit dignity or all have rights we must respect, or, even,
that this is—intuitively or otherwise—the right thing to do) that are always
secondary to the reality of our own reactions and not to be confused with
them.[29]

   When the parable calls this to the lawyer's attention, however, it also,
by doing so, calls him, as it calls us, to a human community our reaction
reflects and one to be formed in part in a conversation about our reaction
and about the parable itself. "This being true for us," the parable says,
"how are we"—you and I, initially, but, as we saw, the issues are always
inevitably social—"to go on?" Given what we now know about ourselves
who are we? How is our community formed? What shape does it take?
What character does it offer to us and how do we, by accepting the
authority of this character, shape it in return? And how can this shaping
work if we are, as we are, a product of this community? Although we are to
be guided in these inquiries by the authority of what has been displayed by
it, the parable itself, as we have seen, does not answer these questions. It

---

[27] See, Malcolm, *supra* note 9 at 91-92.

[28] See, Malcolm, *supra* note 9 at 82.

[29] I am making this point here only for its pedagogical implications. There is,
however, an anthropology, a psychology, and a philosophy of this approach dating
back, at least, to Vico if not to the pre-Socratics. It is one, I believe, that can be
readily associated with the latter Wittgenstein. See Giambattista Vico, *The New
Science of Giambattista Vico*, ed. and trans. by T.G. Bergin and M.H. Fisch (Ithaca:
Cornell Univ. Press).

can't, any more than I can explain what a good metaphor means without destroying its metaphoric meaning.

In *all* our teaching, we, too, like the parable, introduce, invite, and initiate our students to particular human communities constituted by particular human conversations in which we ask that they, the students, find character. At our best, I believe, we do this, as the parable does, by focusing attention upon the human mystery that each of our subjects truthfully is, when observed anew, and starting our thinking there in our reaction to this mystery.

But, surely, this cannot be true for *all* subjects, for how, for example, could we possibly see in the activities that are the sciences something that could be disorientingly re-presented to students in such a manner that would generate inquiries making relevant the relationship of all a student is to the subject? The quotation from Wittgenstein introducing this concluding section, however, is there to justify my use of the word "all." For even mathematics, economics, or Wittgenstein's logic can be taught by starting, again as the parable does, by learning how to observe the details of these activities candidly.[30] We can, for example, ask of each of these three: Why do we have such an activity? What is the community of each like and why is it like that? What does being like this mean for its relationship to other communities of discourse? To what other communities does each community turn for justifications, since it must justify itself and, thus, it must turn to others. How does each community define itself for itself and how does it do so for others? Should others assent to the offered definition? Who is considered within each community such that his or her work "counts"? Who is not? Who is to decide this? When? How? Should others assent to these determinations as well? What words and symbols are used by each? How do these words and symbols come to have the meanings they do? What effect do these meanings have on the similar words and symbols of others? By what processes do these meanings change, as meanings always do? What is to be considered persuasive in arguments within the conversations that

---

[30] Much of what follows in this paragraph, I have learned how to say from reading a truly remarkable book, Joseph Vining, *The Song Sparrow and The Child: Claims of Science and Humanity* (South Bend: Univ. of Notre Dame Press, 2004).

constitute each community, and what is it about certain people that makes them more persuasive in these arguments than others? Who and what is trusted within each community? Why? How are the arguments within each to be presented for the assent of others, as they must be if the activity and the community are to continue? What character does each community form and what form does its authority over those within it take? How do this character and this authority relate to those of other communities? And, lest one think that mathematics, hardest of sciences that it is, is somehow different: How many repeated calculations will be deemed "enough" for confirmation, and by whom, so that calculation itself can continue?[31] Who will decide this? When? How?

In this focus upon the human details of these three subjects, we can readily see, I think, the openings through which human mystery can be revealed and, in this, the openings for true learning about them. If we can, however, open these three subjects to the possibility of starting our study of them in our own reactions to them—if it is possible, that is, to see in these three a half-dead man by the side of the road—how much more so is this true for the softer sciences or the social ones like the law in which my own teaching is found?

Is this not, then, a question of learning and of teaching how to observe the world? I have said all I wanted to say and now conclude with yet another question. Wittgenstein, famously, wished for us that we would view the world as miracle. [32] Even aside from my biblical sources, have I not suggested that all true teaching is inherently religious: an ancient under-standing that perhaps we can learn to see again and anew? Is this so because when we seek to describe true teaching, any true teaching, truthfully we

---

[31] "In certain circumstances we consider a calculation to be sufficiently checked. What gives us the right to do so? Experience? May that not have deceived us? Somewhere we must finish with justification, and then there remains the proposition that we calculate like this." Ludwig Wittgenstein, *On Certainty*, Ed. G. E. M. Anscombe and G. H. von Wright, trans. G.E. M. Anscombe (Oxford: Blackwell Publishing, 1969), 212.

[32] See, Edwards, *supra* note 9 at 91-2 and 234-238.

have no words for our descriptions that are not also religious ones like the one to which Wittgenstein resorted? And, if so, what are we to make of this? What does this say to *any* institution of "higher learning?"[33]

[33] My thanks to Robert Cochran, Dan Edwards, Linda Edwards, Lanier Sammons, Sorrel Sammons, Tom Shaffer, and Michael Smith, for their comments on an earlier draft and to John Dunaway for so gracefully stewarding the Lilly Foundation-funded symposium for which this essay was written. My thanks as well to my responders and the members of the audience at the symposium whose good thoughts, challenges, and encouragement prompted me both to work harder and to see in the essay more potential than I had before.

CHAPTER SIX

Pluralism at a Baptist University

By Andrew Silver
Mercer University

In 1722, a nineteen year-old Jonathan Edwards ventured forth from his isolated Connecticut village to Manhattan Island, a thriving cosmopolitan seaport. There, the future author of "Sinners in the Hands of an Angry God" became a minister of a small Presbyterian church, living with friends in a house near the docks and studying the Bible for months on end, sitting before his western window. When he looked up from his studies, Edwards could peer into the eastern window of the neighboring house, where he saw a Jewish man, deep in prayer. "I once lived for many months next to a Jew," he wrote later, "and had much opportunity daily to observe him; who appeared to me the devoutest person that ever I saw in my life; great part of his time being spent in acts of devotion, at his eastern window, which opened next to mine, seeming to be most earnestly engaged, not only in the daytime, but sometimes whole nights."[1] What Edwards saw in all probability was a bearded man, a Spaniard, in a black cap, a cream-colored prayer shawl, twisting thin black bands of leather seven times around his left forearm, chanting prayer, lifting his arms and wrapping his head in his shawl from time to time, folding himself into God, emptying his soul of world, of self, of everything but the unnamable that remains. Edwards saw a man communing with his creator, laboring with God much as Edwards labored with his God, awaking at 4:00 a.m., studying and writing until his morning walk along the wild banks of the Hudson River, followed by more prayer and study. What Edwards saw in

---

[1] George M. Marsden. *Jonathan Edwards: A Life* (New Haven: Yale University Press, 2003) 46.

that Jewish man was his own commitment to the transcendent mirrored in another human being: what he saw was another soul's version of his own hard love.

It was a precious, delicate moment. What did Edwards do with it? Beyond spectral evidence, beyond vision alone, did he connect himself to this other? Did Edwards throw open his window to listen to the keening prayers coming from the Jewish man's window? Did he enter into dialogue, conversation with this stranger? Did he break bread with him? Did he learn the language, the tradition, the professed truth, of this devout Jew–the "devoutest person" that he ever saw in his life? When he passed him on the street, did he call to him, "Brother!" and greet him; did he look into his eyes?

No record of any other action save observation and acknowledgment remains. The moment closed. Many years later, Edwards would call other religions "false and pernicious" and write that he looked forward to the "overthrow of Judaism, Mahometanism, and heathenism through the world."[2] He could not bring himself to ask questions of this Jewish man any more than the Jewish man could bring himself to ask questions of Edwards the Puritan. Both lived parallel lives of faith in two separate universes. In 1722, they could easily avoid one another and still more easily consign the other to eternal damnation for worshiping God in an unfamiliar way, in a different language, an alien form. Edwards was educated at a religiously orthodox Yale University in the 1720's—he never studied Judaism or Islam or Buddhism or Hinduism—so of course he would call them false and pernicious, the religion of infidels. The closeness of the houses notwithstanding, the windows so tantalizingly near to one another, the window to the east, never opened, the window to the west never opened, the territory between them a universe unexplored. Each to the other is simply pantomime religion—a form, a shadow, gathered at a distance. Edwards's momentary admiration here is converted into fear, fear into disgust, and disgust into dismissal. His strong urge to respect, the urge to dialogue, the urge to love, fought back as treason to true faith. A great moment is lost.

This is the world of exclusivism—a world in which there is only one

---

[2] Marsden, *Jonathan Edwards*, 485.

truth, and our tradition has got it, our denomination has got it. The exclusivist responds to the world's variety and increasing inter-connectedness with the solidity of sure boundaries, with often beautiful but rigid belief. Jonathan Edwards, one of America's greatest exclusivist theologians, saw the world in terms of a religious battle, between "a nation God had favored with true religion versus peoples in Satan's grip, Cath-olics and pagans." The mere approach to another, the curiosity to learn, is seen as a threat to all that is holy.[3]

In a recent lecture on my campus, a speaker referred, in passing, to the deep beauty of Muslim and Jewish forms of vocation. Jonathan Edwards would not have been pleased. The speaker's appreciation of Islam and Judaism probably offended some exclusivists in the audience, for whom such talk borders on heresy. After discussing his appreciation for these faith-traditions, he then noted that Christianity, "of course," has the *highest* form of vocation. He never elaborated upon this claim, but simply expected his largely Christian audience to assume that this was only natural. Theirs might be valuable, but ours is best. Theologians call this way of thinking "inclusivism." Inclusivists acknowledge truth in other religions, but argue that the most perfect form of truth, the highest truth, and the best way to the divine can only be accessed through their home religion. Rather than seeking knowledge in the unfamiliar in other religions, inclusivists are reassured by the most familiar elements of other faith-traditions, which are easily assimilated into one's own beliefs and attributed, in some form, to one's own faith-tradition. Inclusivism holds that, while truth might be found in many religions, there is a hierarchy of religions with only one denomination or faith tradition at the top.

Inclusivists sometimes argue that those in other religions unwittingly worship a God that they simply call by a different name. Christians might say that, when a Hindu venerates Vishnu, Vishnu is really a stand-in for Christ. C.S. Lewis explains: "I think that every prayer which is sincerely made even to a false god... is accepted by the true God and that Christ

---

[3] Marsden, *Jonathan Edwards*, 485.16; For a discussion of exclusivism, inclusivism, and pluralism, see Diana L. Eck. "Is Our God Listening?" In *Encountering God: A Spiritual Journey from Bozeman to Banaras* (Boston: Beacon Press, 1993) 166-200.

saves many who do not think they know him."[4] Theologians call this form of inclusivism "fulfillment theology:" The germs of the fullest religion are found in all religions, but find final expression only in one. In a recent B.C. cartoon by Johnny Hart, a seven-branched Jewish menorah is shown reshaping itself into a cross, each of its seven branches disappearing, its lights extinguished in the final panels, its entire existence subsumed and replaced, made obsolete by the cross. The final words of the cartoon appear just before the replacement of the Jewish menorah by the Christian cross: "It is finished," the panel reads.

If Edwards leaves the Jewish man in his separate house, never approaching closer in his encounter, in the inclusive approach, whether the worshiper knows it or not, he or she is no longer in an adjacent house, but rather unwittingly, a guest in someone else's more perfect house. As a Jew, I am simply a stunted Christian, an anonymous Christian, await-ing full development in Christianity, when my Judaism would be sloughed off like an old and useless skin. As Muslims, your reverence for Mohammed is simply misplaced reverence for Christ. Salvation might be possible in your case because Christ knows that you worship him in a different guise. And Christians, for Jewish inclusivists you too are the chosen people, your worship of Jesus a misplaced adoration of Yahweh. Other religions here are poured into the mold of our own faith-tradition, on our terms, not theirs. Inclusivism is a kind of gentle erasure of other faith-traditions. But at least it's gentle. When I asked an Indian student in one of my classes if she would feel insulted if a Christian were to tell her that there was truth in Hinduism because it was simply worship of Christ through false forms, she said, "that'd be nice compared to what they say about me now!" That's progress—at least she's not an infidel.

In my own approach and search for truth, I've been both an exclusivist and an inclusivist. I grew up in a Reform Jewish household. I attended Hebrew school when I was ten or eleven and was taught about Judaism by women with numbers branded into their wrists by Christians in a Christian country. I was taught not only to be wary of Christianity, but to view Christianity as a threat to my own culture and tradition. For Mrs. Samson, the Holocaust survivor, Christianity was an unknown—something

---

[4] Quoted in Diana L. Eck, *Encountering God* (Boston, Beacon Press: 1993) 179.

"other," something misleading, and a source of iniquity to Jews. I was taught that a second Holocaust could happen at any moment. I was taught to be especially leery of Arabs, who naturally hated Jews, and I was taught nothing at all of Islam. This is the stance of exclusivism—an understandable reaction to horror wreaked upon an entire faith-tradition.

Still, I was curious. Something in me resisted the comfort of exclusivism. Something in me wanted to peer over the walls. Since I was a bit of a trouble-maker in school, my teachers' warnings about other faith-traditions just stoked my curiosity. I remember getting thrown out of Hebrew class for bad behavior and going to the front office to see the principle—a kind, hunched man with an impossibly white moustache named Mr. Schimmel—and I would ask him questions about Judaism and about other religions. I don't remember any of his answers and I don't remember any of my questions, but I remember that, for the first time, the act of questioning about tabooed subjects was seen as special. Mr. Schimmel saw my restlessness and curiosity as something to cultivate.

When I got to college, I began taking classes on world religion. I took Old Testament (for me, simply the Hebrew Bible), New Testament, Western Religion, Eastern Religion, American Religious Traditions, Theory of Religion, Hinduism, Medieval Judaism, and a five-course progression in Christian history. I did not approach Christianity as a student with the idea that it represented an inferior form of religion; I approached Christianity looking for truth as an equal. I developed a hunger both for that which was familiar to me in other religions–the reverence for the transcendent, the restless search for truth, the advocacy of justice at cost of self, the need for repentance and atonement—but also I hungered for that which was unfamiliar: the idea of radical non-violence, of maya, of karma, of reincarnation. This was a scary period for me. Not only was I displaced from my homogenous suburban hometown, attending school in a Washington D.C. teeming with a poverty and homelessness that challenged my commitment to justice, but I was also displaced from the exclusivist shape of my faith-tradition as I entered into dialogue with other faith traditions. To move from an I-It relationship to an I–Thou relationship is uncomfortable, it's agitating, it stirs up. It was a frightening thing for me as a Jew to study world religion, and to confront the truth of other religious traditions. I had, for at least a few months, during the study of world religion, a crisis of identity—a kind of spiritual vertigo. My thoroughly assimilated American sense that the self mattered most, that the self was central in my life, received a shock, a jolt.

My orthodox Jewish great-grandfather might have, had he been living, thought of this period in my life as a dangerous period of disbelief, of straying from the fold of Judaism, of taking seriously the words of infidels like Buddha and Jesus and Mohammad. He might have viewed this, with horror, as a threat to my Judaism. But the truth is that this brief period of statuslessness, this time of anxiety and uncertainty, this moment of radical openness, signified a broadening of my spirit, not a loss of it, and that these growing pains made me a far more considerate Jew, a far more engaged Jew than I would have been had I never felt the approach of another's divinity, had I never opened my soul to other faith-traditions and felt their impress on my own faith. This made my faith a much less comfortable, a much more strenuous, a much more complex affair. I did not abandon Judaism; I abandoned unexamined Judaism. These experiences called me out of myself, made me acknowledge and love that which was different from my faith tradition, even while broadening and deepening my own Judaism. I was agitated. I was made restless for truth. I entered college a Jew who assents, and I came out a Jew who searches. My deep encounter with other faith-traditions didn't kill my Judaism, it resurrected it; it resurrected me. And these encounters continue to resurrect me.

Unbeknownst to me I had become a pluralist. I didn't have a scarlet "P" on my graduation robe; it didn't say "pluralism" on my diploma. I didn't even know what pluralism meant. Even now I don't consider myself a "Pluralist." It sounds too prescribed, too creedal, too easy, too trendy–too much like some new dogma that requires my assent. I had simply, by the end of my education, become somebody who, anchored in my own faith-tradition, sought out encounters with other faith-traditions, not to annihilate them or condemn them, not to assimilate them or replace them, but for loving conversation, for dialogue, for listening. Angela Davis, an African-American scholar and a former Black Panther, explains: "I'm convinced... that we have to find ways of coming together in a different way, not the old notion of coalition in which we anchor ourselves very solidly in our communities and simply voice our solidarity with other people. I'm not suggesting that we do not anchor ourselves in our communities... but I think that to use a metaphor, the rope attached to that anchor should be long enough to allow us to move into other communities to understand and learn.... What I'm interested in is communities that are not static, that can change."[5] In college, I had learned to stretch the rope attached to the anchor, and in so doing I was able to discover new expressions of the truth in new communities even while becoming more aware of the bedrock in which my faith-tradition is anchored. Pluralism, Diana Eck writes, "assumes both openness and commitment," both a search and a home for that search.[6]

So for me to answer the question of pluralism in a Baptist university, I might first speak as a Jew, from experience, about what pluralism would mean at a Jewish university. I would want a good foundation in the history of Judaism, in the Hebrew Bible for young Jewish students. But I would never want Jews to graduate from a Jewish university without encountering other faith-traditions on those traditions' own terms. I would not want students to leave a Jewish university without listening to another soul's love of the divine. I would not want Jewish students to leave a Jewish university without being agitated, in the best sense, by other faith-traditions. I would hope that a Jewish university would go out of its way to recruit Jewish and non-Jewish faculty, and even more importantly, non-Jewish students. I would reluctantly embrace one class that covered every single non-Jewish faith-tradition, from Christianity to Islam to Hinduism to Buddhism, all covered within a fourteen- or fifteen-week semester, but I'd be happier still to see individual classes taught by scholars in these religions, in which students might encounter these faith-traditions at a yet deeper level, just as I was able to do at the Methodist university I attended. The endowment for my university would be quite large. My colleague and friend Michael Cass has written a musical anthem for our First-Year Seminar program, a blues song that asserts that the aim of a good education is to "create a disturbance in your mind." I would hope that Jewish students might be creatively and constructively disturbed. I would not have a cloistered college. I would not have a college cut off from dialogue with other faith

---

[5] Quoted in Anna Deveare Smith, *Fires in the Mirror* (New York: Anchor Books, 1993) 32.

[6] Eck, 193.

traditions. I would not want a college in which Jews would define themselves as above or opposed to other faith traditions. And in order to embrace the other, there need to be others around to embrace. It's one thing to love the ideas of another culture, it's another to love people from other cultures. And diversity alone does not equal engagement. For a few months in New York City, Jonathan Edwards was confronted with diversity and his response was to observe it from afar, but approach no nearer to another soul. Without the attempt to know other faith traditions, diversity asks nothing of us, calls nothing from us. One cannot only retreat into the self to understand the other.

What would pluralism at a Baptist university look like? I can't tell you. That wouldn't be true to Baptist belief and it wouldn't be true to pluralist belief. Pluralism is found in dialogue, not monologue, and so I listen deeply and I speak in conversation. Rick Wilson[7] speaks of the need for "soul competency–the responsibility to read scripture in a community of freedom... everyone must have the liberty to find that God. This is not a foundation-less pluralism," he tells us, "it is a pluralism that rests upon a foundation that allows a search." President Godsey writes in his essay that "we are not discrete organisms... our beliefs are not discrete beliefs, they share, just as our DNA, with other human communities... we are nothing without the human embrace of the other that lies deep within us. We belong to one another." Until we have learned to love other faith-traditions and until we learn to see from other perspectives, inclusion remains a judgment made without embrace, without love. I listen to my brother in the English department, Gordon Johnston, a Christian who loves Buddhism, among other faith-traditions, who says: "I've yet to find a faith or a practice that did not help me as father, poet, partner, and (in the largest sense) brother. My experience is that enlarging one's reverence is never damaging, because enlarged reverence is enlarged ability to love." And, a good Baptist turned Methodist Buddhist, he quotes the Catholic monk Thomas Merton to me: "Love takes one's neighbor as one's other self, and loves him with all the immense humility and discretion and reserve and reverence without which no one can presume to enter the

---

[7] Richard F. Wilson, Chair of the Christianity Department at Mercer University.

sanctuary of another's subjectivity. From such love all authoritarian brutality, all exploitation, domineering, and condescension must necessarily be absent."[8] As a Jew, I listen and I call that Catholic truth beautiful and it calls me out from myself. This love must be part of a Baptist education. In his essay, "The Meaning of a Baptist University,"[9] Dr. Godsey explains that the "freedom to speak carries with it the responsibility to listen," arguing that we must have in our learning experience both "openness and integrity." To cover one's head in a shawl, to immerse oneself in one's Bible, to engage in renunciation as a virtue, in self-isolation, is part of almost every religion, and it is a great part of the beauty of religion; but to emerge from beneath that shawl, to pause from reading biblical passages, and to walk outside to fill the soul with the love of others, to fold oneself into communities outside one's own, actively to listen and actively to love, all of this must also be part of our religion and it must be part of our education.

Nearly three hundred years after Jonathan Edwards's encounter, we live in a many-windowed world. Will we be content to watch from the safety of our room the pantomime religiosity of others? Will we retreat into our house, shutter the windows, bar the door? Or will we dare to extend ourselves beyond the doors of our homes and love what is beautiful and true without? Jonathan Edwards experienced his first inward dwelling of spirit out of doors, walking, looking up to the sky and clouds, overcome by what he called a "sweet sense of the glorious majesty and grace of God, that I know not how to express." That God transcends human expression is one of the great truths of pluralism. We must have the humility to know that God is bigger than our idea of God. After his conversion experience, Edwards wrote, "the appearance of everything was altered: there seemed to be, as it were, a calm, sweet cast, or appearance of divine glory, in almost everything. God's excellency, his wisdom, his purity and love, seemed to appear in everything, in the sun, moon and stars; in the clouds, and the blue sky; in the grass, flowers, trees; in the water, and all nature. ... I often used to sit and view the moon, for a long time; and so in the daytime, spent much time in viewing the clouds and sky, to behold the

---

[8] Thomas Merton, *The Wisdom of the Desert* (New Directions, 1960) 18.
[9] Unpublished pamphlet printed by Mercer University.

sweet glory of God in these things." This is what Gordon Johnston calls Edwards's Buddhist moment, and Dr. Johnston reminds us that there is "pluralism in non-human listening too." We could do worse, it seems to me, than to foster Edwards's spirit of renunciation, of humility, of devotion, but also to turn Edwards's love of nature on our fellow humans: to look on our fellow human beings as sun, moon and stars; as clouds and blue sky; as grass, flowers, trees; as water. We can do worse than to see the "sweet Glory of God in these things," to throw our windows open, venture forth from our houses, visit other people's homes, feel awe at their sacred architecture, break bread with them, call them brother, come back to enrich our homes, and venture forth again. In all religions, in all education, in all, we should be, as Walt Whitman put it, "enamour'd of growing outdoors." As Gordon Johnston explained, "There is always another, fuller personhood at which to arrive." There is always another resurrection.

CHAPTER SEVEN

What Makes Church-Related Education Christian?

By Richard T. Hughes
Pepperdine University

The 1990s witnessed a plethora of books and articles exploring the thesis that the Christian dimension of church-related higher education has been in steady decline from the late nineteenth century until now.[1] That thesis inevitably raises the question of this essay: "What makes church-related education Christian?"

I want to address the question by posing a two-fold thesis of my own. The first part of my thesis is this: If a church-related college or university aspires to serve as a *Christian* institution, the very first requirement is for that college or university to ground every aspect of its work in a theological frame of reference.

Pragmatic considerations, so common in merely church-related education, are insufficient to drive enrollment decisions, marketing decisions, curricular decisions, and decisions that bear on student life. To be sure, no institution can escape pragmatic considerations. At the same time, Christian colleges and universities should ground *all* strategic decisions in a shared theological vision. Without that dimension, a church-related college or university can hardly claim much depth as a Christian

---

[1] The work of George Marsden and James Burtchaell is particularly noteworthy in this regard. See George Marsden, *The Soul of the American University: From Protestant Establishment to Established Nonbelief* (Oxford: Oxford University Press, 1994); and James Tunstead Burtchaell, *The Dying of the Light: The Disengagement of Colleges and Universities from their Christian Churches* (Grand Rapids: Eerdmans, 1998).

institution.

Stanley Hauerwas affirmed in his Gifford Lectures for 2001 that the question for him was "not whether a university can be Christian, but whether a church exists sufficient to sustain a Christian university."[2] Hauerwas's question highlights the fact that denominations content to function without a richly textured theological tradition will likely never sponsor schools that move much beyond the category of church-relatedness, even though they may call their colleges "Christian."

The second part of my thesis takes the form of a paradox and is meant to explore the kind of theological framework that can sustain a genuinely Christian college or university. On the one hand, I want to argue that church-related education is most deeply Christian when it reflects a radical commitment to Christian discipleship. On the other hand, I want to argue that church-related education is most deeply Christian when it reflects a radical commitment to diversity, pluralism, and genuine academic freedom, and grounds that commitment in a Christian vision of reality.

In fact, I will bracket this discussion with reference to two books that, on the face of things, seem to stand poles apart from one another. One is Lee Camp's *Mere Discipleship*, an uncompromising call for cross-centered living in the twenty-first century. The other is Daniel Taylor's *The Myth of Certainty*, a book that seems to undermine radical claims of any sort, including Camp's embrace of what he calls "radical Christianity." But I am convinced that these two books, together, provide a wonderful basis for answering the question, "What makes church-related education Christian?"

ORIENTING OURSELVES THEOLOGICALLY

I want now to illustrate my thesis by exploring two theological traditions that, yoked together, have the potential to sustain a seriously Christian college or university. Both those traditions descend from the sixteenth century. One is the theological perspective of Martin Luther. The other is the theological perspective of the sixteenth-century Anabaptists.

To claim that these two traditions might work together in a common

---

    [2] Stanley Hauerwas, *With the Grain of the Universe: The Church's Witness and Natural Theology* (Grand Rapids: Brazos Press, 2001) 233.

enterprise may seem like the strangest paradox of all, since Luther and the Anabaptists were so completely at odds. They quarreled over the legitimacy of the state church. They quarreled over the question of infant baptism. And they quarreled over the proper role of works in the life of a believer.

Their quarrels were so intense that the Anabaptists often viewed Luther as a compromiser and no serious Christian at all. For his part, Luther thought the Anabaptists had embraced a doctrine of works righteousness that essentially nullified the good news of the Christian gospel. In addition, Luther viewed their rejection of the state church as fundamentally seditious. He therefore joined Zwingli, Calvin, and the Catholic hierarchy in calling for their destruction.

Yet, Luther and the Anabaptists shared one thing in common: they both were profoundly radical. Historians often single out the Anabaptists as the true "radicals" of the Reformation, but Luther could hardly have been more radical when he pressed his position to the wall with statements like this:

> Then do we do nothing and work nothing in order to obtain this righteousness? I reply: Nothing at all. For this righteousness means to do nothing, to hear nothing, and to know nothing about the Law or about works but to know and believe only this: that Christ . . . is our High Priest, interceding for us and reigning over us and in us through grace.[3]

Luther even suggested that "should he [a Christian] grow so foolish... as to presume to become righteous, free, saved, and a Christian by means of some good work, he would instantly lose faith and all its benefits."[4]

The fact is that Luther claimed the doctrine of justification by grace through faith in the most radical way possible, while the Anabaptists claimed the doctrine of sanctification in the most radical way possible. It is hardly any wonder that these two traditions have been at odds for the better part of 500 years.

While the divorce between Luther and the Anabaptists is hardly

---

[3] Martin Luther, *Lectures on Galatians, 1535* in Jaroslav Pelikan, ed., *Luther's Works*, vol 26 (Saint Louis: Concordia Publishing House, 1963) 8.

[4] Martin Luther, *Freedom of a Christian*, 1520, in Harold Grimm, ed., *Luther's Works*, vol. 31 (Philadelphia: Fortress Press, 1957) 356.

surprising, it also stands as one of the greatest tragedies in the history of the Reformation. For that rupture was more than a divorce between two Christian movements. The split between Luther and the Anabaptists also meant that the seamless robe of the gospel was torn in two. For 500 years Luther and his heirs have carefully nurtured the doctrine of justification by grace through faith, while the heirs of the Anabaptists have made discipleship the hallmark of a truly meaningful faith.

When all is said and done, however, the doctrine of justification and the doctrine of sanctification are two sides of the same Christian gospel. Luther's advice to "sin boldly" and the Anabaptists' advice to "take up one's cross" are complementary expressions of the same Christian tradition. Luther's insistence that no one can possibly be good enough to save one's self squares beautifully, if paradoxically, with the emphasis the Anabaptists placed on a lifestyle of radically selfless living.

Lest one imagine that the split between Luther and the Anabaptists might have been avoided had each side been content to moderate its claims and embrace a more conservative version of its message, let it be said that both were right in pressing their respective emphases in bold and compelling ways. The doctrine that Christians are justified by grace through faith is an incredibly radical claim, and Luther would have done that doctrine a gross disservice had he preached it with moderation. Likewise, the Christian call to sanctification is a radical demand for cross-centered living. Had the Anabaptists turned that demand into the suggestion that Christians embrace cross-centered lives merely *up to a point*, or had they sought to conform that doctrine to the cultural norms of a fallen empire, they would have lost entirely the meaning of the biblical doctrine of sanctification.

I am suggesting, then, that both these themes—justification and sanctification—are all-or-nothing propositions. But the fact that they are all-or-nothing propositions means that, when yoked together as they are in the Christian gospel, they form an extraordinary paradox. I am also suggesting that these two sides of the Christian paradox, if embraced simultaneously, can provide the strongest possible foundation for a church-related college or university to live out its Christian commitments in a consistent and holistic way.

What would that suggestion look like if implemented on the ground?

I want to explore that question by taking up, first, the doctrine of sanctification and, second, the doctrine of justification by grace through faith.

SANCTIFICATION AND CROSS-CENTERED LIVING

The biblical understanding of sanctification leads inevitably to the notion of discipleship—even radical discipleship—for the call to sanctification is not a summons to "be nice" or to "be moral" or to "be respectable." Rather, the call to sanctification is a summons to cross-centered living.

David Lipscomb, the Anabaptist-like nineteenth-century leader of Churches of Christ and co-founder of the school that eventually became Lipscomb University in Nashville, Tennessee, put it well when he wrote, "There is no doubt the devil is willing to turn moral reformer and make the world moral and respectable." But from Lipscomb's perspective, morality and respectability were insufficient. Instead, Lipscomb claimed, the New Testament advocates "a full surrender of the soul, mind, and body up to God," leading to "the spirit of self-denial, of self-sacrifice, the forbearance [sic] and long suffering, [and] the doing good for evil."[5]

Samuel S. Hill Jr.—the dean of historians of religion in the American South who labored for most of his career in the University of North Carolina and the University of Florida—once told me that, in his view, church-related higher education could become again a powerful force in American life. But for that to happen, he said, Christian colleges and universities would have to be less content to be merely church-related and more concerned to recover the radical implications of the Christian gospel.

What might it mean to recover the radical implications of the Christian gospel?

To help answer this question, I want to turn to Lee Camp's insightful book, *Mere Discipleship: Radical Christianity in a Rebellious World*. Camp argues that Christians practiced a radical form of faithfulness to the teachings of Jesus for the first 300 years of Christian history. They shared their possessions with those in need, rejected violence, and sought to live out the values of the Upside-down Kingdom.

---

[5] David Lipscomb, *Civil Government*, 1889 (Nashville: Gospel Advocate, 1957) 144-45.

But all that changed in the fourth century when Constantine legalized the Christian faith and when Theodosius made Christianity the official religion of the Roman Empire. From that time on, the church served the empire even as the empire protected the church, and the notion of radical discipleship—with precious few exceptions—was lost.

Camp argues that while the Constantinian compromise is ancient history, many American Christians nonetheless view the world through a "Constantinian cataract."[6] Many, for example, view themselves as *American* Christians whose first allegiance is to the United States, rather than as Christians who happen to live in the United States and whose first allegiance is not to America but to the Kingdom of God.

For such Christians, "empire" defines reality, Jesus and his teachings become impractical and irrelevant to the "real world," and serious discipleship essentially disappears. Christians who define their identity in terms of empire, Camp argues, inevitably serve the goal of self-preservation. They therefore trust in the power of the state, the power of the market, and the power of the sword, rather than in the power of the cross that requires disciples to abandon themselves for the sake of the neighbor, even if the neighbor proves to be an enemy.

On the other hand, radical discipleship means that Christians render to the Kingdom of God their complete and unqualified allegiance, even if that allegiance entails suffering. For Christians who find the notion of suffering unsettling, Camp points out time and again that the cross—not power and privilege—defines the Kingdom of God.

From this perspective, Camp explores the biblical meaning of nonviolence. "Christians refuse to fight wars," he explains, "not because they naively believe they will thus rid the world of war; instead, we do not fight wars because the kingdom of God has come, in which war is banished, in which it is possible to order our lives according to the justice and peace of God. Christian non-violence, then, is always rooted in the narrative of redemption."[7]

In that context, Camp explores what he calls "the political meaning

---

[6] Lee Camp, *Mere Discipleship: Radical Christianity in a Rebellious World* (Grand Rapids: Brazos Press, 2003) 21.

[7] Camp, *Mere Discipleship*, 127.

of baptism." In baptism, Camp explains, "Christians become part of a community that transcends all racial, cultural, national, geographical, and natural boundaries." Conversely, "the god of 'God and country' does not baptize into the Spirit of Christ, but the spirit of homeland security; this god baptizes not in the blood of the Lamb, but the blood of soil and country."[8]

Even a cursory reading of American history reveals the extent to which American Christians have often viewed the world through the "Constantinian cataract" that Camp describes. In the nineteenth century, for example, Frederick Douglass, the noted abolitionist and former slave, argued that American Christianity had so thoroughly conformed itself to the norms of the broader culture, and especially the norm of slavery, that it no longer resembled the teachings of Jesus. In 1845, as he concluded his autobiography, Douglass wrote the following words:

> Between the Christianity of this land, and the Christianity of Christ, I recognize the widest possible difference—so wide, that to receive the one as good, pure, and holy, is of necessity to reject the other as bad, corrupt, and wicked. To be the friend of the one, is of necessity to be the enemy of the other. I love the pure, peaceable, and impartial Christianity of Christ; I therefore hate the corrupt, slaveholding, women-whipping, cradle-plundering, partial and hypocritical Christianity of this land. Indeed, I can see no reason, but the most deceitful one, for calling the religion of this land Christianity. I look upon it as the climax of all misnomers, the boldest of all frauds, and the grossest of all libels.

And then, so no one could imagine his quarrel was with southern churches only, Douglass concluded, "Dark and terrible as is this picture, I hold it to be strictly true of the overwhelming mass of professed Christians in America."[9]

One hundred and eighteen years later, Martin Luther King Jr. picked up on the very same theme. In his "Letter From a Birmingham Jail," King lamented the extent to which Christianity in the American South had become little more than a reflection of cultural tradition. "In the midst of blatant injustices inflicted upon the Negro," he wrote, "I have watched

---

[8] Camp, *Mere Discipleship*, 145.
[9] Frederick Douglass, *Narrative of the Life of Frederick Douglass, An American Slave, Written By Himself*, 1845 (New York: Signet Books, 1968) 120-21.

white churches stand on the sideline and merely mouth pious irrelevancies and sanctimonious trivialities. In the midst of a mighty struggle to rid our nation of racial and economic injustice, I have heard so many ministers say, 'Those are social issues with which the gospel has no real concern.'" Then King wrote,

> On sweltering summer days and crisp autumn mornings I have looked at [the]... beautiful churches [of the South] with their lofty spires pointing heavenward. I have beheld the impressive outlay of her massive religious education buildings. Over and over again I have found myself asking: "What kind of people worship here? Who is their God? Where were their voices when the lips of Governor Barnett dripped with words of interposition and nullification? Where were they when Governor Wallace gave the clarion call for defiance and hatred? Where were their voices of support when tired, bruised and weary Negro men and women decided to rise from the dark dungeons of complacency to the bright hills of creative protest?"[10]

For King, radical Christianity didn't conform to the values of the culture; it conformed itself to the mandates of the gospel, and on the basis of the gospel, stood in judgment on the culture with its moral and ethical compromises.

The question we now must raise is this: what does this extended discussion of radical Christianity have to do with church-related higher education? We can answer that question by asking another: If King had examined the church-related institutions of higher learning in the South—schools like Mercer, Xavier, Furman, Samford, Lipscomb, Rhodes, Baylor, Davidson, Harding, Hendrix, Southern Methodist, Wesleyan, or Abilene Christian—would he have judged those institutions in the same way that he judged their sponsoring churches?

I can tell you this. I was an undergraduate student at a church-related institution in the South between 1961 and 1965. For all those years, I was no more than 250 miles from most of the great events of the Freedom Movement. The lunch counter sit-ins had begun the year before I entered college and continued throughout my undergraduate years. In 1963, midway through my undergraduate experience, Martin Luther King led hundreds

---

[10] Martin Luther King Jr., "Letter From a Birmingham Jail" in James M. Washington, ed., *I Have a Dream: Writings and Speeches that Changed the World* (San Francisco: HarperSanFrancisco, 1986) 96-97.

of children through the streets of Birmingham, protesting racial segregation. The city responded with fire hoses and police dogs. In 1965, the year I graduated from college, blacks sought to march across the Edmund Pettus Bridge from Selma to Montgomery, but Alabama storm troopers stopped them in their tracks with shockingly brutal force.

Unbelievably, in spite of the fact that one of the greatest moral dramas in the history of the United States was unfolding under my nose, I missed it. I missed it almost entirely. I didn't fully discover what I had missed until I enrolled as a graduate student at the University of Iowa in 1967. I blame myself, but I also blame that church-related college and its professors, for not one of my teachers said to me, "What is going on today is important. Take note." Or better still, "Get involved."

Should my professors have encouraged me to take the Freedom Movement seriously? Should they have urged me to participate? Given the purposes of higher education—and Christian higher education in particular—could it have been their rightful role to encourage in my classmates and me an openness—even a commitment—to the claims of discipleship in the context of the Freedom Movement? Could it have been their rightful role to encourage us to judge the culture by the light of the Christian gospel instead of the other way around?

It is well enough to talk about issues like slavery in the nineteenth century or the Freedom Movement that took place almost half a century ago, but the real question for us is this: What is our responsibility as teachers when faced with comparable moral issues today? For example, do we engage our students in an exploration of how the Christian faith might bear on the war in Iraq? Do we help them explore what the Christian faith might say regarding war and violence in any context at all? In a culture where a majority of students are chiefly concerned with making money and living the good life, do we encourage our students to embrace the values of the Upside-down Kingdom? Do we counsel them to take Jesus seriously when He told us to lose ourselves for the sake of others; when He told us to invite to dinner the poor, the maim, and the blind; when He told us to die in order to live; or when He told us to take up the cross and follow Him? Do we explore with our students what all this might mean in the context of their lives and their vocations?

On the other hand, has the Constantinian cataract so obscured our vision that our practice of Christian higher education has been chiefly shaped by our allegiance to the empire rather than to the Kingdom of God?

Someone might well ask, "What possible justification could there be for bringing a consideration of discipleship and sanctification into our classrooms?" We can answer that question easily enough.

Over the past twenty years, many scholars in church-related colleges and universities have concluded that Christian faith and secular learning should, indeed, connect in significant ways. The dominant paradigm for that connection has increasingly become the integrationist model that calls for the "integration of faith and learning."

As good as that model may be, it has its deficiencies. In an important book called *Teaching Peace*, produced in large part by Mennonite scholars at Bluffton College, Gerald Biesecker-Mast argues that the integrationist model is deficient in part because it begins with the creation rather than with the life and teachings of Jesus. It can therefore sidestep the radical claims of the Christian gospel, and can do so quite easily. Precisely for that reason, as Biesecker-Mast explains, the integrationist model "is usually mobilized on behalf of conservative rather than liberationist social agendas, sometimes explicitly rejecting the more radical Anabaptist critiques of social and political systems."[11]

In another important book—*Scholarship and Christian Faith: Enlarging the Conversation*—Rodney Sawatsky, president of Messiah College, argues that when proponents of the integrationist model speak of faith and learning, they typically narrow "their definition of faith to mean religious *beliefs about* God, the world, and humankind, or a *worldview* embracing all these ideals [italics mine]." But what about "faith as a verb?" Sawatsky asks perceptively. What about "faith understood as trust" or faith understood as "'seeking and discovering meaning'?" And what about "hope" and "love"? After all, he notes, "The Apostle Paul used three words to describe the full contours of Christian identity: faith, hope, and love." Sawatsky then argues that in addition to integrating learning with faith

---

[11] Gerald Biesecker-Mast, "Christian Nonviolence and the Enlightenment Crisis" in J. Denny Weaver and Gerald Biesecker-Mast, eds., *Teaching Peace: Nonviolence and the Liberal Arts* (New York: Rowman and Littlefield, 2003) 7.

understood as a noun, Christian scholars should also integrate learning with hope, with love, and with faith understood as trust or a search for meaning.[12]

In this highly suggestive passage, Sawatsky offers a powerful rationale for integrating the virtues of faith, hope, and love into our teaching and our scholarship. He thereby provides us with compelling reasons for teaching discipleship, sanctification, and cross-centered living, even as we teach history, literature, anthropology, and physics.

To this point in our discussion of sanctification, however, we have told only half the story. The second part of the story—every bit as critical as the first—pertains not so much to teachers and scholars as to high-level administrators and development officials at church-related colleges and universities and to the way they market their institutions.

It is not uncommon for faculty members at these colleges and universities to work diligently at connecting their teaching and their scholarship with Christian faith and discipleship, while the development staff pulls the institution in completely different directions. This can happen, for example, when a school seeks to market itself as a Democratic institution or a Republican institution as opposed to a Christian institution, or when development officers confuse the way of the cross with American ideals, nationalism, and patriotism.

There is a great deal of money to be raised from people who think of the United States as a Christian nation and who confuse discipleship with patriotism, but the church-related college or university that embarks on that path does so at the risk of great peril. The fact is, my own under-graduate institution—the church-related school that did such a good job of sheltering my colleagues and me from the Civil Rights Movement—held as its official motto the phrase, "Where Christian and American ideals go hand in hand." Is there not irony here?

The fact is, Christian and American ideals are often incompatible. The liberty that the Declaration of Independence holds to be an "unalienable right," for example, is often construed as the liberty to

---

[12] Rodney J. Sawatsky, "Prologue: The Virtue of Scholarly Hope" in Douglas Jacobsen and Rhonda Hustedt Jacobsen, eds., *Scholarship & Christian Faith: Enlarging the Conversation* (New York: Oxford University Press, 2004).

pursue one's own self-interest, while liberty in the context of Christian faith is the liberty *from* self-interest and the freedom to give one's self away. Capitalism values acquisition, places a premium on greed, and encourages citizens to say of their possessions, "This is mine." Christian faith, on the other hand, maintains that all things are God's, that nothing is finally "ours," that we are only stewards of the earth, and that we must share the wealth that comes into our hands with those less fortunate than ourselves. One could go on and on with the contrasts between American ideals and institutions and the meaning of the Christian call to discipleship.

In spite of these contrasts, however, some church-related schools sell themselves as schools that are committed to a predominantly American vision of reality, and some colleges and universities that market themselves as Christian institutions still court donors who confuse the Christian faith with the American way of life. The crucial consideration here is that donors, quite understandably, typically give with the expectation that the institution that receives their gift will embrace their values. To that extent, all institutions are donor-driven.

An undergraduate student once told me that she had been invited to make a report to a group of donors who gave generously to an unnamed church-related college. She was shocked to hear these donors insist that the school in question recruit "more Republican students" and "make the school a bastion for conservative politics." One might wish that those donors had argued for more Christian students who were willing to embrace the biblical call to discipleship.

In order to be true to its mission, it is crucial that a Christian institution find donors who share the values of the gospel, rather than donors who bring a perspective alien to the gospel and who seek to shape the institution according to their own ideological commitments.

In our attempt to answer the question, "What makes church-related education Christian?" we have focused to this point on one side of the Christian paradox—the doctrine of sanctification—and we have explored that doctrine's implications for teaching, for scholarship, and for institutional development. Now we must turn to the other side of the Christian paradox—the doctrine of justification by grace through faith.

JUSTIFICATION BY GRACE THROUGH FAITH AND THE MANDATE FOR DIVERSITY, PLURALISM, AND ACADEMIC FREEDOM

In the introductory section of this chapter, I stated the following: I want to argue that church-related education is most deeply Christian when it reflects a radical commitment to Christian discipleship. On the other hand, I want to argue that church-related education is most deeply Christian when it reflects a radical commitment to diversity, pluralism, and genuine academic freedom, and grounds that commitment in a Christian vision of reality.

The Christian vision of reality in which church-related colleges and universities can ground their commitment to diversity, pluralism, and academic freedom is, quite simply, the biblical doctrine of justification by grace through faith. That doctrine presupposes two important themes.

First, it presupposes that God alone is God. He is the infinite Lord of heaven and earth, the one whose love no one can fathom and whose goodness and greatness no one can comprehend.

Second, it presupposes that human beings, while made in God's image, are nonetheless finite, frail, and subject to extraordinary limitations—limitations underscored by the fact that death is a fundamental and inescapable dimension of human life. Our finitude means, among other things, that our knowledge is limited and our understanding is flawed, simply by virtue of the fact that we are human beings, confined to a particular time and a particular place. Even if we were to expand our horizons through study and travel, we would never completely overcome the limitations that define our lives. Not only this, but greed and self-interest—traits that define the meaning of sin—inevitably cloud our vision and limit both the scope and accuracy of our perception. Given these extraordinary limitations, how could we possibly imagine that we could save ourselves?

These two themes—the sovereignty of the infinite God and the finitude of humankind—give meaning to the doctrine of justification by grace through faith. God has said "yes" to us by virtue of His infinite love and grace. We are asked to accept that grace through the light of faith.

These two themes—the sovereignty of the infinite God and the finitude of humankind—also provide the strongest possible motivation for a Christian college or university to embrace diversity, pluralism, and academic freedom.

If it is true that our knowledge is limited and our understanding flawed simply by virtue of time and place, and if it is true that greed and self-interest inevitably cloud our vision and limit the scope of our perception, then who are we to insist that we alone have a corner on the market of truth? Who are we to assume that other human beings from other cultures, from other periods in human history, from other political persuasions and other religions may not have perceptions and understandings fully as valid as our own?

This consideration means that of all educational institutions, Christian colleges and universities stand under a mandate to embrace diversity and pluralism and to extend to their faculties the freedom to search, to think, and to explore, even when those explorations threaten our sense of self and render us less than comfortable. This is precisely why I wish to argue that church-related education is most deeply Christian when it reflects a radical commitment to diversity, pluralism, and genuine academic freedom and grounds that commitment in a Christian vision of reality.

Daniel Taylor, in his remarkable book, *The Myth of Certainty*, sheds abundant light on this issue. As a young man growing up in a fundamentalist church, Taylor discovered, much to his chagrin, that his fellow Christians typically prized both certainty and orthodoxy, and prized them in oppressive ways. He struggled with the fact that he was not allowed to question the church, its beliefs, or its practices. He discovered that "questioning the institution . . . [was] synonymous, for many, with attacking God."[13]

Years later as a graduate student, and then as a young professor, he discovered the same oppressive reality in the context of the American academy, except the academy substituted secular orthodoxies for religious orthodoxies. Further, he discovered that those who embraced those secular orthodoxies often punished those who dared to question their legitimacy. "Reflecting critically on secularist orthodoxy," he wrote, "will draw just

---

[13] Daniel Taylor, *The Myth of Certainty* (Downers Grove: InterVarsity Press, 1986) 30.

as much fire in this world, which supposedly prizes reflection, as questioning religious orthodoxy will in the other."[14]

Warned of orthodoxies that must never be questioned and truths that must never be doubted, Taylor embarked on a long, intense struggle with the entire question of certainty. He shares both the struggle and the conclusions he finally reached in his book, *The Myth of Certainty*.

His essential conclusion, as the title of the book suggests, is that certainty is, indeed, a myth, especially when certainty pertains to absolutes. "Absolutes, by definition, partake of infinity," he writes. "They are without boundary. What relationship can a finite knower have with an infinite object of knowledge except a finite, limited one? Can one then be said to know or 'have' an absolute on which to ground one's beliefs when one only knows, at best, a sliver of that absolute?"[15]

Indeed, Taylor makes a strong case for radical skepticism. The reflective Christian does well, in my view, to freely admit the possibility of being wrong. All I believe in may in fact be false. God may be only wish fulfillment. The sense of His presence that I sometimes get in worship and prayer may derive simply from the release of certain chemicals in the brain. Those occasions where He seems to have guided my life may only be coincidence or reflect my human desire to find a pattern in events.[16]

On reading a passage like this, someone might well ask in what sense Taylor can claim to be Christian at all. If he is willing freely to "admit the possibility of being wrong" and seriously to entertain the notion that even his belief in God "may be only wish fulfillment," how on earth can Taylor claim any credible Christian allegiance whatsoever?

In response, Taylor writes that his Christian convictions rest not on certainty, but on faith. What is this, but an affirmation of the historic Christian doctrine that we are justified by grace through faith, and not by works, knowledge, or certainty? "Faith," he writes, "is a quality and a choice consistent with the riskiness of the human condition. It is an appropriate response to the world as I find it."[17] Put another way, Taylor

---

[14] Taylor, *The Myth of Certainty*, 49.
[15] Taylor, *The Myth of Certainty*, 91.
[16] Taylor, *The Myth of Certainty*, 97.
[17] Taylor, *The Myth of Certainty*, 98.

embraces his finitude. What else can he do? Indeed, if we admit that our vision is clouded and distorted by time and place, self-interest and greed, what else can anyone do?

Taylor's assertion that "the reflective Christian does well... to freely admit the possibility of being wrong," strikes me as a modern counterpart to Luther's confident assertion that the Christian inevitably sins. Luther advised his followers to accept their humanity, their finitude, and their brokenness, and therefore to "sin boldly." In like manner, Taylor counsels Christians to accept the fact that final certitude is a myth and, therefore, to doubt boldly, since doubt is the inevitable counterpart of faith.

"There is no more honest expression of the tension of faith," Taylor claims, "than that of the distraught father in the gospel of Mark seeking healing for his child. To Jesus' assertion that belief makes all things possible, the father cries out in tears, 'Lord, I believe; help thou my unbelief.'"[18] In Taylor's judgment, this distraught father is a stand-in for every person who faces the question of certainty about ultimate things.

> Taylor concludes his book with this assertion. The goal of faith is not to create a set of immutable, rationalized, precisely defined and defendable beliefs to preserve forever. It is to recover a relationship with God.... As a belief system, the Christian religion is subject to the many ills of all belief systems; as an encounter with God, it transforms individual lives and human history. God does not give us primarily a belief system; he gives us Himself, most clearly in the person of Jesus Christ, so that truth and meaning can be ours through a commitment to that love with which He first loved us. The risk is great, but the reward is infinite.[19]

We now must ask, what does this discussion of doubt, faith, and certitude have to do with the task of Christian education? How does it contribute to any meaningful answer to the question, "What makes church-related education Christian?" And finally, how does it relate to the other half of the Christian paradox, the demand for radical discipleship?

Already, I have suggested that a frank acceptance of our radical finitude, and the frank acceptance of the fact that we are justified not by works or knowledge or wisdom, but by God's infinite grace, is a powerful

---

[18] Taylor, *The Myth of Certainty*, 98.
[19] Taylor, *The Myth of Certainty*, 123-24.

foundation—and a profoundly Christian foundation—on which a Christian college can build an institutional commitment to diversity, pluralism, and academic freedom.

Second, a frank acceptance of our radical finitude, and the frank acceptance of the fact that we are justified not by works or knowledge or wisdom, but by God's infinite grace, should make us cautious about dogmatisms of every kind, even dogmatisms regarding radical discipleship. We live by the light of faith, and what may be clear to me may not be so clear to my brother or my sister.

Further, recognition of our finitude should make us sensitive to the ambiguity of the human situation. No situation is ideal and no circumstance is perfect. This is a profoundly Christian teaching, and a teaching that means, quite frankly, that the Christian must be prepared for compromise. For example, the Christian institution that seeks to identify donors who are fully in sync with the institution's mission may find donors who are on board in certain ways but not in others.

The wise administrator, the wise development officer, will have to make a determination regarding how much compromise the institution can tolerate in a given situation, while still maintaining the integrity of the institutional mission. But the genius of the wise and committed administrator of a Christian college or university is this: He or she will always chart the vessel's course by asking, "How does this or that decision square with the basic theological convictions that undergird this institution? How does it square with the institution's commitment to discipleship? How does it square with our confidence in the grace of almighty God?"

These conclusions, in turn, should cause those associated with Christian higher education carefully to nurture a profound sense of humility regarding our work and to avoid at all costs any hint of triumphalism. After all, Christian schools, like all human institutions, are fundamentally flawed. What makes the difference in Christian higher education are the commitments that under-gird and inform our work—the commitment to a radical sense of discipleship and the commitment to the good news that God's love sustains us even in the midst of our failures.

CONCLUSIONS

If acceptance of our finitude and recognition of the ambiguity of the human situation should make us cautious about dogmatisms and open even to compromise in certain situations, why then would I say—as I did say earlier in this essay—that the Christian doctrines of radical discipleship and justification by grace through faith are, each of them, all-or-nothing propositions?

The truth is, they *are* all-or-nothing propositions, and precisely here we find the paradox of the Christian gospel. The demand for radical discipleship is a categorical imperative, to be sure, but it never cancels out the absolute message of grace. Paul makes this point when he tells the Galatians, "All who rely on observing the law are under a curse, for it is written: 'Cursed is everyone who does not continue to do everything written in the Book of the Law.' Clearly no one is justified before God by the law, because, 'The righteous will live by faith.'" (Gal 3:10-11)

At the same time, the absolute reality of God's grace does not constitute license to ignore the categorical imperative to discipleship. After his tribute to the power of grace, Paul then asked the Roman Christians what really amounted to a rhetorical question.

> What shall we say, then? Shall we go on sinning so that grace may increase? By no means! We died to sin; how can we live in it any longer? Or don't you know that all of us who were baptized into Christ Jesus were baptized into his death? We were therefore buried with him through baptism into death in order that, just as Christ was raised from the dead through the glory of the Father, we too may live a new life. (Gal 6:1-4)

The truth is, the gospel *is* a radical message. It is radical in its call for discipleship and radical in its promise of grace. But grace apart from discipleship can be "cheap," and discipleship apart from grace can quickly degenerate into legalism. This is why sanctification *and* justification are the two indispensable poles of the paradox of the Christian gospel, and the two indispensable dimensions of Christian higher education.

When the board, the administration, and the faculty of a church-related college or university can embrace this paradox and orient the institution squarely in the context of these imperatives, that institution ceases to be merely church-related. It becomes, instead, deeply and profoundly Christian.

CHAPTER EIGHT

The Calling of the Teacher and the Place of Community

By David Lyle Jeffrey
Baylor University

"...vocation... draws us together."
A.J. "Chip" Conyers

In historic Christian discussions of vocation two types are typically distinguished: a general call to faith and obedience (e.g., Matt. 22:14; Eph. 4:4-16; Phil. 3:14-17) and special, even extraordinary callings to particular acts or forms of service (e.g., Ezek. 2:3ff.; Acts 9:10-18). The first call is universal in the sense that it is experienced by all who profess faith; the second is often highly specific and usually related to what in the secular sense we have lately come to think of as career, or "profession." Colloquially, it may be said that all those who are "happy in Jesus," as the old hymn has it, are happy in pretty much the same familial way: trust and obedience in following this call leads to communal blessing in the here and now, and then, as part of the "company of the blessed," superlatively so in the hereafter. The second order of vocation is often highly specific, and though typically related to career, or "profession," implies likewise a possibility that there will be need for a still more acute self-transcendence. A call to particular and perhaps even extraordinary duty—what in contemporary parlance is sometimes rather quaintly called "leadership"—can in practice lead to tasks that can seem to be in tension with—even almost to contradict—the call to a common happiness.

As in biblical narratives, the "duties of one's calling" vary widely in the character of their challenge or preoccupation, so it may be said of

Christians with a keen sense of personal "vocation" that each is likely to be drawn out and challenged in a distinctive, particular fashion. Just because a special call proves both authentic and irresistible, it does not follow that responding to it will necessarily produce a delirium of personal bliss; even as the celebrated assurance that in the end "all shall be well" does not mean "all shall be happy," or the biblical adage "it is good to obey" guarantee that such "good" will, in the experience, turn out to be "just the way I'd like it." What *should* follow from an authentic sense of special, personal calling is a deep conviction—and eventual confirmation—that the call was authentic. This is all that we are promised and, in the biblical view of things, all that is really necessary. A further difficulty with a special sense of calling is that it may or may not be recognized by other folk with whom one has to share the work. Academic administrators, I suspect, may well on this account feel a certain lonely empathy for the recalcitrant Moses, or with old Abraham, who, as Hebrews 11:8 tells us, was obedient to his call, "not knowing where he was going." (Faculty members who serve under them, on the other hand, may for perfectly understandable reasons entirely lack such empathy for the old buzzard, while agreeing firmly upon the need for a better map.)

Unfortunately, where special calling is concerned, it can get to be far less flattering than sometimes we imagine. Holy Scripture itself is filled with warnings that the second order of calling--to a specific instrumental purpose--does not necessarily imply that the person called has, at the time, a particularly meritorious complement of intellectual or moral achievement. However counter-intuitive, it is instructive to consider that Jephthah the intemperate, Barak the timid, and Rahab the prostitute all make the honor roll (Heb. 11:32), not to mention characters like "Cyrus, my servant" (Isa. 44:28-45) or "Assyria, the rod of my anger," (Isa. 10:5) who wreak a havoc of God's wrath on his own elect. John Milton observes the usual distinction succinctly:

> It is by *general* vocation that God invites all men to a knowledge of his true godhead. He does this in various ways, but all of them are sufficient to his purpose.... *Special* vocation means that God, whenever he chooses, invites certain selected individuals, either from the so-called elect or from the

reprobate, more clearly and insistently than is normal.[1]

In this classic view (let the called beware), the sense of special vocation that is our common subject in this volume all too apparently carries with it a potential for fractious deviation or even exemption from the redemptive grace that characterizes the first, or general calling of the believer! Not for nothing does Paul confess to the Corinthians that he constrains himself by rigorous personal discipline, lest in fulfilling his calling he forfeit grace and become a "castaway." (1 Cor. 9:27)

Awareness of these matters can create anxiety in someone who takes the notion of vocation (in either sense) seriously. At the very least, it becomes impossible to overlook tensions that may exist between the two categories of "call." Further, whereas the general calling upon all believers seems everywhere to privilege community life (e.g., Heb. 10:25; Acts 1-2, etc.), those upon whom the second order of vocation falls with a vengeance—biblically one may think of prophets such as Jonah, Amos, Jeremiah, Ezekiel, or John the Baptist—often seem chosen despite that by nature or nurture they are personality-averse to a public life, even agoraphobic. I do not mean to suggest that professors are at all like prophets, merely that, however loosely, one sandal fits: Academics quite often have personality profiles that dispose them rather awkwardly toward the gregariousness and conviviality of the classroom.

I hasten to confess to my readers, *cum granum salum*, that I must probably count myself among the apparent misfits. Family and close friends readily concur with the assessment of a pair of seminary survivors who, to amuse themselves, once ran a Myers-Briggs test on me and gleefully pronounced me an incorrigible "INTP." When I asked what that meant, one said with a laugh, "Basically, it means you are—ahem—unsuited to your job." Uncertain though I remain about the technical niceties of psychometric classification, what "INTP" seems to amount to is something like "introverted nerd, totally perplexed." Yet, as a university teacher, my calling requires of me daily almost the opposite disposition—or at least quite a bit more than what comes to me naturally. To respond adequately to my calling in the classroom requires therefore a kind of self-

[1]John Milton, *De Doctrina Christiana*, *Complete Prose Works*, Ed. D.M. Wolfe et al. 8 vols. (New Haven: Yale University Press, 1953-1957) 6:455.

transcendence and sometimes discomfort. Yet it is the discomfort, frankly, that has had most to teach me about the deeper meaning of "special" vocation, and I suspect this may be true of others.

I. *APOLOGIA*: THE GRAIN OF SALT

Vocation is not necessarily co-incident with discovering our natural aptitudes or confirming our natural pleasures. Two or three years ago I was boarding a flight from Dallas to Atlanta and felt, almost physically, an intense, impatient set of glaring eyes behind me in the aisle. A tall, tough-looking woman, dressed from head to toe in black and with hair as blond as bleach could make it, clearly wanted me out of her way. (Perhaps permanently, for all I could tell—her glare had real poison in it.) I sat down quickly. As I did so I noticed that she had rings and other objects of metal not only in her ears, nose and lips, but through her cheeks and eyebrows. As she jostled and jammed her luggage into the overhead rack next to my seat I suddenly was eyeball-to-navel with a bare midriff similarly festooned with alien metal, and saw just above it on her black shirt an iridescent message: "Pierced in Places You Will Never See." I had hardly begun to contemplate the possible significance of this message when it occurred to me with alarm that she was eyeing the empty seat beside me. I am sure my reflexive "Thank the Lord!" was almost audible, and I was extraordinarily grateful as she took the seat directly behind me instead.

Almost immediately, however, I was burdened by a familiar guilt. There are still occasions on which I want with all my heart to flee what might well be simply an opportunity to "exercise my calling," just because it challenges my 'comfort zone.' I am using "calling" here, of course, in the first sense, as those raised in a Baptist church in particular are wont most often to use the term (cf. 2 Thess. 1:10-12). Because of the typical individualism of Baptists, however, translating this universal order of our calling can be blunted (in rugged extroverts as well) by various modes of self-preoccupation—or self-preservation. Some of this, I allow, can be culturally "justified." Other elements are more difficult to explain coherently or consistently with a biblical notion of calling.

Anthropologists tell us that it is possible to learn a great deal about a people through observation of their signature games. If an anthropologist had happened in upon Wednesday night youth group in the church I grew up in, he would have realized almost immediately that the signature game at Calvary Baptist was musical chairs. Studied carefully, it would have revealed everything an anthropologist might want to know about our kind of Baptist polity, Baptist courting rituals and, ultimately, Baptist theology.

As many of my readers will remember, it works like this: chairs are set in a line, initially with one for each participant. Then the music starts--in our case on an old record player on which the favorite musical-chairs recording was by the Blackwood Brothers quartet. One chair is removed as the game begins. Everyone circles the line of chairs in tense anticipation. There is considerable jostling for position. At any unlikely point, the music is stopped in its tracks, and all rush to sit down. Whoever doesn't make it goes to the wall—and so on, *seriatim*, till only one is left.

The perennial champion at musical chairs in my youth group was a young woman named Rosemary. She was physically strong—a woman of substance, so to speak—and her low center of gravity already stood her in good stead on the women's hockey team on which she had achieved a certain distinction for a formidable hip-check. To capture a sense of our Wednesday night rituals, what you must imagine is the old Blackwood Brothers singing "Would you be free from your burden of sin (bump), There's power in the blood, (bump), Power in the blood" (thump)..." with Rosemary at every line-end hip-checking some gangly teenaged boy smack-up against the wall like a rubber chicken. By the end of the game that's where we all were—by comparison with her prowess just so many stringbeans in a chorus line of defeat—while she sat, grinning and sweatily triumphant, on the last chair. I still have an old black-and-white photograph of her like that, elbow on her knee, hand under her chin, invincible.

We boys weren't actually as dejected as you might imagine. Already we all knew the deeper rules: musical chairs might be the last thing at our church someone like Rosemary would ever win. We would grow up to be the bubbas in the boardroom, while down in the basement Rosemary would be stirring spaghetti for the potluck afterward. She comes to my mind once in awhile. She stopped coming to church; I have never actually seen her since graduation, and no one seems even to know now where she lives.

But I suspect she too, in quite another fashion, may be pierced in places you and I will never see.

I mention this memory because it has played a part in my own "special" calling to teach and, especially, to study the way Scripture gets interpreted by culture. Working in this field over a lifetime has led me to a conviction that, no more than the general calling to follow Christ, can the special calling to be a teacher be lived out responsibly by an individualist, rugged or otherwise. Each, to answer to the definition, must be understood as a call to community, to others. There is something inherently self-defeating in that extreme *post-hoc* pressure on the logic of the Reformation by which we find ourselves, at last, with the music ended, metonymically in a church of one.

Let me also confess openly that I have no singular expertise when it comes to the subject of calling. I have had no theophanic moments in my own life; you may take my word for it that no bush has ever taken spontaneous fire in my presence, and—teenagers in our house notwithstanding—I don't usually hear voices in the night. Accordingly, the thesis of this essay is as open as any other academic essay to falsification. I have, however, read and absorbed like blotting paper the writings of numerous intellectual Christians, and among them are voices that now also resonate in my memory, continually instructive. It turns out that the majority of these thinkers regard vocation (in both species) in biblical terms, hence as unavoidably a call *out of self and into relationship* with a wider world of persons to whom one's call must, in some fashion, be related. In other words, these teachers of the ages see both general and particular vocation as a call to service. This point may seem obvious enough, therefore, not to need restating, but in our academic culture, I am convinced, it warrants more thinking about.

II. THE BIBLE AND INDIVIDUAL VOCATION

A recurrent pattern is apparent already in the biblical call of Moses, first of the *nab'im*, or prophets (Heb. *nab'i*, derives from vb. *nabu*—to call.) For him, the bush really did burn. He clearly did not want to accept his commission, and in the Exodus account he tries every strategy to escape it: He insists he isn't qualified (Exod. 3:11); no one will believe his call to be authentic anyway (4:1); and he lacks the requisite eloquence (4:10). Anyone else would be better (4:13). But sent he is, all the same; qualifications are not, for the biblical prophets at least, even a matter up for discussion. Nor, as I have already suggested, is there evidence of any extraordinary intelligence of the prophet in most cases: Jeremiah, seeking to evade his own call, is hapless enough to plagiarize the excuses of Moses almost verbatim: "Ah! Lord God! Behold I cannot speak, for I am a child" (Jer. 1:7), but, it must be noted, to equally nugatory effect. Prophets in the Bible are, after all, mere mouthpieces, not at all the artistic visionaries that the Romantic poets Shelley or Blake imagined (Isaiah perhaps excepted). All a prophet has to do, once called, is show up. (As the negative example of Jonah makes clear, for a prophet, not showing up can produce unpleasant consequences.)

Unfortunately, however, with a special calling to the academic life things tend not to be so apodictically straightforward. Just showing up will not suffice. Among other things, acquiring some order of capacity for public speech is generally a good idea. Further, there are the encumbrances of an appropriate academic training in a discipline (prophets require no such formal training) and, finally, being more or less at ease with the surprisingly conformist eccentricities of a pedagogical lifestyle is undeniably a positive indicator for probable academic success. (I am inclined to believe it helps if the postulant can already be comfortable in an out-of-fashion tweed jacket or the feminine equivalent.) But as the call of Lady Wisdom, the street-teacher of Prov. 1-9 rather eloquently suggests, there is for *every* would-be teacher an absolutely *sine qua non* requirement: genuinely positive response to an invitation to life-long learning. For such ongoing learning to occur, community is indispensable.

Moreover, when experienced by real individuals it also seems clear enough that the process of responding to such a "calling" is not entirely consistent with an evaluation by reduction to pure "rational choice." Our thinking about future academic possibilities while we are yet students, for instance, is generally prompted by something that seems vaguely appealing, but as yet, in its deeper realities, still pretty much unknown. The most compelling "argument" for us may be little more than our admiration for one or more of our own teachers, and gratitude for the way they have enriched our lives. But these people may be very different from us in experience, personality or talent in ways that make our appreciation for their contribution no real assurance that we will have comparable satisfactions in a life of teaching.

There seems to me no reliable way around this bed of nettles. As in other situations, responding to a calling—which may also be described in secularist language as a "vocation"—may at some crucial juncture involve responding to an imperspicuous, non-self-evident good, and only in the process of obedience to the call can it be truly known as a good. We are obliged to step out in faith. This can be a little like receiving a proposal of marriage, and just about as daunting. Many of us don't much like to have to assent to the full consequences to know a promised good.

Yet, while this element of risk-taking is not equivalent to simply making a "rational" evaluation of gifts, skills, and the pertinence of a given educational formation, then calculating their value to a proposed professional occupation, it does not preclude such evaluation. It is appropriate that rational evaluation and, ideally, community accord, confirm even a strong vocational impulse—especially where personalities so risk-averse and hence information-dependent as typical academics are involved. For all that, at the end of the day, responding to the impulse requires a decisive individual conviction, "personal" in the most radical sense, all the residual unknowables notwithstanding.

III. AUGUSTINE ON INTELLECTUAL VOCATION

St. Augustine's extensive discussion in his *Confessions* of his own call—first to faith and then to teaching—has often provided a post-biblical *locus classicus* for Christian intellectual reflection on the meaning and process of both categories of vocation. One reason is his transparency about the normal human tendency to rationalize, even to the point of self-delusion, as we work our way through momentous questions and their attendant decisions. He sees that everybody's theory (whatever the subject) is at least partly autobiographical and, accordingly, that accurate establishment of the truth about our own affections is crucial early on in the process. In his view, we must make the effort truly to confess who it is we are in ourselves before we decide accountably what it would mean to confess Christ, let alone bear him witness in a specific vocational context.

Otherwise, in us the light of Christ would soon become gravely darkened by the obtrusion of ego.

For Augustine, vocation is the result of an educational as well as a spiritual journey. At the age of 19 he was first intellectually "converted" to the life of learning through reading a lost book of Cicero's called *Hortensius* ("The Gardener"). This book, he says, changed his "outlook on life," even his prayers to God, and provided him with "new hopes and aspirations."[2] Suddenly there welled up in him a new and intense order of affection for truth (3.6) and accordingly a love of justice (3.7). These affections themselves prompted many challenging philosophical questions, e.g., are Truth and Justice absolutes? Or are they projections, merely, of language and culture (3.8)? That is, ought they to be regarded merely as shadowy manifestations of subjective human preferences, projections of a given social consciousness or personal will to power? Or are truth and justice, like our longing after them, inherent in the very order of Creation itself?

But the effort to answer such intellectual questions was far from extrinsic to his subsequent conversion to Christianity. This too came by the mediation of a book (St. Paul to the Romans). In the mysterious and apparently incidental call (*"Tolle lege, tolle lege"*) to take up and read the Scriptures in his search for truth he later came to see a deeper call to accept not only the lordship of Christ but the fellowship of believers, the Church as in-common teacher of the experience of faith (Book 8). Intellectual vocation thus became wedded to spiritual vocation in Augustine's experience; it is discovered to be the result of a self-conscious act of the will in response to an understanding of the "call" embedded in both personal and community narratives—our own personal story and the "grand narrative" we come to share.

That an account such as Augustine's (a similar example is C.S. Lewis's *Surprised by Joy*) should reverse the polarity of progression experienced by many Christian intellectuals—in which personal faith *precedes* special vocational calling (e.g., John Milton, George Herbert, Isaac Watts, Jonathan Edwards, William Faraday, Alvin Plantinga)—only serves to

[2] St. Augustine, *Confessions*. tr. R. S. Pine-Coffin (Hammondsworth, UK: Penguin, 1961) 3.4.

sharpen our sense both of the distinction and yet eventual need for integration of the two species of calling. It doesn't in the end seem much to matter, in order of time, whether a calling to the intellectual life precedes or follows the call to Christian life. What matters is that in attempting obedience one call is not held aloof from the other.

An essential feature of Christian core convictions about the value of the individual person and therefore of the appropriateness of special calling relates fundamentally, nevertheless, to an order of value in which our corporate calling to be the body of Christ in the world (cf. Rom. 12; 1 Cor. 12) is clearly pre-eminent. The Church is one body, with many diverse members, and these members are both created for a diversity of roles and accorded a diversity of spiritual gifts (1 Cor. 12:8) in order that the whole body may be built up, or, as it says in the English of the King James translation, "edified"(Eph. 4:12). Conversion does not require a denial of particular gifts, social standing, or educational experience: St. Paul goes so far as to encourage the young Corinthian believers to stay in the calling in which they were called (1 Cor. 7:20); he means that the general calling to Christ transcends the issue of vocation in its narrower sense (1 Cor. 7:24). The point is that all particular vocation is—or may be— redeemed in relation to the shared life in Christ, if indeed it is offered up to Christ and the service of his Body in the world. This view of the calling of the Church is thus, with respect to special vocation, pluralist, leading Augustine to observe, "I saw that the Church was full, yet its members each followed a different path in the world" (8.1). In this breadth of perspective he echoes views of some of the early Fathers, such as Clement of Alexandria, who writes: "Since we are convinced that God is to be found everywhere, we plough our fields praising the Lord, we sail the seas and ply all other trades singing his mercies."[3]

If the sanctification of ordinary work was expected to be a consequence of one's calling to faith, the consecration of ordinary work performed subsequently was thought to be natural to all Christians. Later, the motto *laborare est orare* ("to work is to pray") would mark the Benedictines' attitude to a specifically set-apart religious life in an enclosed

---

[3]Clement of Alexandria. *Stromateis*. J.P. Migne, ed. (Paris: Patrilogia Graeca, 1866), 9.45; reprint—(Ridgewood, N.J.: Gregg Press, 1965), 7.7.

community. In its early centuries, the Church was typically more relaxed about the issue of special personal vocation than subsequently Christians were wont to be. It is Augustine probably more than any other post-biblical writer who makes careful discernment of personal vocation a burning personal issue for subsequent centuries.

IV. FROM THE MONASTERIES TO *MIDDLEMARCH*

In early medieval Christian tradition the question of vocation typically arose, as it did for Augustine, in respect to the call to monastic life. In its essence, this call was an invitation to leave one form of community behind (a community in the world) in order to enter another community, far more rigorous in its demands upon individuals to relate to the common good. (There was nothing less sacrosanct in medieval monasteries than individual space or "privilege.") Scripturally, the Acts of the Apostles (2:38-47) hovers in the background. Within the monastic community discernment of sub-vocation was also practiced: some became vintners, others shepherds, cattle-keepers, iron, and tinsmiths, herbalists, scribes, estate managers and the like. Yet each special calling was still part of an overall calling to a community life that, especially among groups such as the Benedictines, had learning at its core. Monastic libraries became the salvation of classical learning in the West, as well as of early scientific knowledge, even as monastic *scholia* became the origin of the university curriculum. Other analogies continue to be observable in regard to a calling to university life and its various duties today, not the least of which is the way in which a university or college vocation still tends to be much more all-encompassing of the life of its members than is usually the case, say, in the career of a public librarian or tax accountant.

In the age of the cathedral schools, such as at St. Victor in France in the twelfth century, the idea of religious as distinct from secular vocation received further development. The phrase "to have a vocation" begins to become firmly attached to any full-time religious calling, whether to the priesthood, the monastery, or to life as a recluse or hermit. St. Thomas Aquinas a century later devoted three works to a theology of vocation in which the call to one or another species of ordination is what he has in mind (*Contra Impugnantes Religione*; *De Perfectione Vitae Spiritualis*; *Contra*

Retrahentes ab Ingressu in Religionem).[4] By the fourteenth century Walter
Hilton, an Augustinian canon in England, is able once again to draw upon
a less restrictive sense of the concept. Elaborating a threefold distinction
that goes back in some form as far as Clement of Alexandria, he speaks of
the possibility of a "mixed life," neither a call to ordination nor to a purely
secular life, but to a combination of an intense regimen of devotion with
"staying in the calling wherein you were called." Specifically, he endeavors
to dissuade a layman of high status from retreat to a monastery in response
to the intensity of his personal spiritual experience, but rather encourages
him to fulfill his calling in his secular duties in the world.[5]

In Reformation writers, perhaps especially in the former Augustinian
monk Martin Luther, the idea that temporal and spiritual calling are
intimately connected gained further emphasis. Referring to 1 Cor. 7:20,
Luther taught that *all* lawful occupations were divine callings, a conviction
shared by Calvin. Following Calvin, the Puritans, as in John Cotton's essay
"Christian Calling,"[6] came to encourage an astute balance between the
management of worldly affairs and one's mindfulness of what Jonathan
Edwards was later to call "religious affections."

The secular use of "vocation" in a sense of high professionalism is
accordingly both derivative from a term with a rich Jewish and Christian
history and, frequently, a narrow, mechanical substitute for its content.
The concept remains, nonetheless, so thoroughly spiritual in its ambience
that in the biblically literate era of Shakespeare, wisecracks for the
groundlings may safely depend on it. An example is *Henry IV, Part 1*, in a
bit of repartee between Prince Hal and Falstaff:

---

[4] Thomas Aquinas, St. *Summa Theologica*. Ed Nicolai, Sylvii et al. 8 vols.
(Ludovicus: Barri-Ducis, 1873). This continues to be the sense in which the term
"vocation" is understood by most Catholics. Thus, in his *Portrait of the Artist as a
Young Man*, James Joyce parlays a question from the director of the Jesuit college
to Stephen ("have you ever felt you had a vocation?") in which the sense is clearly
a call to ordained priesthood, into Stephen Dedalus's alternate notion of an artistic
"priesthood," in which he will "transmute the daily bread of experience" into art
(ch. 4).

[5] Hilton, Walter. *Epistle on the Medyled Lyf*. Tr. David Lyle Jeffrey, in *Toward
a Perfect Love: the Spiritual Counsel of Walter Hilton* (Vancouver: Regent, 1985),
2001.

[6] ed. P. Miller, 171-81.

Prince: I see a good amendment of life in thee—
From praying to purse-taking.
Falstaff: Why Hal,'tis my vocation, Hal. Tis no sin for a man to
labor in his vocation. (1.2.103-106)

Laborare est orare, indeed.

Thus, though a George Herbert may play on the meaning of "call
ing" almost entirely in reference to its application to religious vocation and
ordination (in his personal vocational poem "The Collar"), alluding crisply
to Jeremiah's excuses in his trenchant, self-admonishing conclusion, it is
the notion of higher, or "spiritual" transvaluation of secular vocation that
tends to receive most attention in later literature. It is this would-be-
transcendent sense that lends irony to the all-too-ordinary loss of
vocational purpose noted increasingly by nineteenth-century writers such
as George Eliot:

> ...in the multitude of middle-aged men who go about their vocation in a
> daily course determined for them in much the same way as the tie of their
> cravats, there is always a good number who once meant to shape their own
> deeds and alter the world a little.[7]

That is, in a humdrum life one may find oneself collared in quite another
fashion than Herbert had in mind, and find a good deal less of redeeming
value in the circumstance. In each case, however, work formally in the
church or work in the world, since calling is inevitably to community, for
anyone self-consciously reflective about it there will be a high order of
obligation to others. As Bob Dylan's song has it, "You gotta serve
somebody" other than yourself—or some mere abstraction, such as "the
intellectual life" or "science," that disguises this fact. The great thing is
above all to serve a higher purpose than mere self-will and the making of
mammon.

V. GETTING IT TOGETHER

Robert Frost has a poem about trying to get together his avocation—what

---

[7] George Eliot, *Middlemarch* (Edinburgh and London: Blackwood, 1875) ch 15.

he does for love—and his vocation—whereby he earns his daily bread. It contains several lines to our purpose:

> My object in living is to unite
> My avocation and my vocation
> As my two eyes make me one in sight.
> Only where love and need are one,
> And the work is play for mortal stakes,
> Is the deed ever really done
> For Heaven's and the future's sake.[8]

Getting together what we do for love and what we do for sustenance seems to me to be pretty much like getting together the first order of our spiritual obligations and our love for the particular craft to which we feel we have been called. And Frost is right: when this happens the work we accomplish is then able to be transformed; it may even become work "for Heaven's and the future's sake"—work as worship, work as service.

It strikes me that a special vocation for any Christian ought to be considered as a call to the "mixed life," a consecration of ordinary work such that it becomes a sacrifice of praise, an act of worship. On this understanding the work is itself a species of worship (in Hebrew *avodah* may refer to either);[9] and each person's work goes together with that of others to make up the "living sacrifice" that St. Paul describes in Romans 12 as the proper service of the whole Body. At the personal level this offering up begins, for Paul, with an intellectual transformation, renewing of the mind (v. 2). It requires self-restraint, notably recognition that each of us is given but a part of what is necessary to the health of the whole

---

[8] Robert Frost, "Two Tramps in Mud Time," *The Complete Poems of Robert Frost* (New York: Holt, Reinhart, 1964) 66-72.

[9] This version of the Benedictines' *Laborare est orare* (the early Benedictines knew no Hebrew) shows how deeply etched into biblical consciousness is the connection. It is still a belief of Hasidic spirituality that one can make mystical contact with God, analogous to that achieved in prayer, while working for one's livelihood, and the language expressing it is indistinguishable from Christian monastic language on the subject: e.g., "Let your worship and your work be a fresh miracle to you every day. Only such worship, performed from the heart, with enthusiasm, is acceptable to God" (Louis I. Newman, *Hasidic Anthology*, 337).

body, evident "intellectuals" included (3-8). Teaching, and the learning that must always precede it are among these gifts; some members have them to a distinctive degree (v. 7) and so are called to put their vocation to learning to use—in exemplary fashion—for the benefit of others. In order to do this work effectively, as the balance of this celebrated chapter of Romans makes perfectly clear, our affections *must* be ordered toward love of the common good rather than toward our own profit. In other words, the real gift is without profit to one who sees it as the means to a singular or individualistic end. Another way to phrase this would be to say that Christians may respond to an individual call, but an authentic call will not be individualistic.

Academics especially need to be self-examining on this point. From the time we are in graduate school, focused with an all-encompassing intensity on our dissertations, on into the early, especially pre-tenure years of our career, we are hyper-conscious of our need to get our research done, our findings written up, and our classes prepared. This is entirely understandable; we cannot even be responsible, let alone successful, without doing this work and doing it well. Consequently, it is all too easy to become resentful of anything that frustrates the sense of urgency we feel about these priorities. Time for students outside of class, time for rich conversation with our colleagues—even time with our friends and families—can all seem at enmity with our quest for success. Nothing could be farther from the truth. If we do not make time for participation in the lives of others our own best thinking, in the end, is likely to become myopic, perhaps to all but a few, incomprehensible or substantially irrelevant. If, as teachers, we are reflexively impatient with anything or anybody who detains us, even momentarily, from what we may find ourselves describing as "my own work", then we are forgetting the ends that our work was intended to serve. In such a case we may be in grave danger of forgetting our calling altogether, having become preoccupied with the means rather than the end, the proper goal of our vocation.

The reader will perhaps think that I began this essay as a Baptist, so to speak, and have now back-slidden, by way of insight from the history of the wider church, to a somewhat more ecumenical reflection. And so I have, I suppose, trying to pay heed to many wise members of the Body of which Christ is the head, learning from each something that may enrich my own sense of calling. It is not only from witnesses from the body of Christ of the past, however, that one may learn, *mutatis mutandum*, such necessary lessons. I have discovered that perhaps one of the most enriching privileges of the academic life is the opportunity to play a part in a vital, ongoing fellowship of scholars from many disciplines, in friendship and often spirited dialogue and debate to have my own categories of understanding as well as my repertoire of intellectual resources challenged, refined and expanded again and again. Interdisciplinary faculty-graduate student reading groups devoted to challenging, category- and vocabulary-stretching intellectual and social consideration have again and again provided oil for my own lamp. Christians from many denominations have been a rich part of my ongoing life of learning, and that is truer now than ever; iron sharpens iron as different viewpoints, each nonetheless in the service of a common ordering of the affections, come together to celebrate the great good of a true community of learning. Here is an experience of common good that those who would be teachers can only know by experience, but they have to know it, I believe, to really flourish in their calling.

I confess to a continuing worry about the penchant in some of my fellow Baptists for a kind of "I-did-it-my way" Frank Sinatra individualism in which the general Christian calling to a common good can get easily compromised—even forgotten altogether. The older, sometimes reflexive Baptist tendency to make a sharp division between the realm of worship and our world of work can easily deny to us the constructive opportunities of a middle ground, in which these goods flow fruitfully together out of our willingness to "love God with all our heart, soul, and mind" and, out of that love in turn, "our neighbor as ourselves" (Matt. 22:37-40). The consecration of our ordinary work, work as worship and as prayer, might lead us to see opportunities for faithfulness in the life of the mind that require of us not so much an exaltation of our own philosophy (to paraphrase Hamlet's rebuke to Horatio) as mere Christian obedience. Such obedience to our first call is a condition without which we cannot be Christian; to our second and specific call, perhaps especially to the vocation of teaching, I believe, obedience to the Great Commandment equally applies (cf. 1 Timothy, ch. 6).

Setting these thoughts down has occasioned in my mind the thought that there has been a prior call of which Christians are necessarily aware, and which I have not at all here discussed. Yet it deserves by far the most serious contemplation, for the other two depend upon it. I refer, of course, to the call answered by One whose name all Christians bear: that Christos who was truly obedient to his calling and in whom, accordingly, was found no darkness at all (Ps. 139: 12; 1 Jn. 1:5; cf. Heb. 1:3). He too was pierced—pierced unto death—but in his case it was for all our sakes, our iniquities, and our healing (cf. Zech. 12:10; John 19:37; Isa. 53). That, more than anything else, is what calls those of us who hear his voice to a *cura pastoralis* of his Body in the world, to the fellowship of his suffering, and for some of us that means patiently—and gladly—to learn and to teach. It would be hard to imagine a greater honor, or one more likely to gladden the heart of a thoughtful Christian.

CHAPTER NINE

Integrating Heart, Mind, and Soul: The Vocation of the Christian Teacher[1]

By Jeanne Heffernan
Villanova University

AUTOBIOGRAPHICAL NOTES

A cradle Catholic, I grew up in a devoutly religious home. As I reflect on it now, various elements of my upbringing testified to the harmony between faith and the intellectual life, to *fides quarens intellectum*. My parents were both trained in the natural sciences and worked as physicians. Each had a deep appreciation for scientific inquiry, though their intellectual horizon was far broader. My mother, for instance, received the Pegis translation of the *Summa Theologica* as a graduation present from medical school (no trip to Cancun for her!), a gift that would foreshadow a life-long dedication to the Dominicans. My father's intellectual curiosity also ran deep. He was an inventor, a sculptor, and an essayist. Both of them were culture-bearers whose love of learning was matched by a keen sense of social concern; together they shouldered the prophetic burden of defending the vulnerable, especially the unborn, for thirty years. Though I didn't recognize it at the time, my parents understood something about living an integrated life, a life in which intelligence and professional training found purpose and expression in discipleship. Somehow, I'm sure by deeds more often than words, my mother and father taught us that the

---

[1] Portions of this essay were published earlier in *The Cresset* or were delivered in lecture form for the Pepperdine Center for Faith and Learning. They have been used here with permission.

heart and mind are essentially connected to the soul.

This connection was evident in the very artifacts of our home. In addition to medical journals and scientific periodicals, our living room featured an array of books on psychology, history, art, and literature—all of which settled in quite naturally among theological and devotional works. Before I knew anything of their significance, I had seen on our bookshelves the names of Erikson and Freud, Cézanne and El Greco, Evelyn Waugh and T.S. Eliot. But I noticed, too, that these names were accompanied by others I had heard in church, names like Ignatius and Thérèse and Thomas More. In the cosmos that was our library, the sacred and the secular both found a place. I recall that the Bible held preeminence, though, as it lay open on one of our tall tables underneath a large crucifix: the Word above all other words.

From early on, then, my home life taught me that faith and learning were natural companions. Despite countless hours of television and other diversions, I was initiated into a Catholic culture of learning. This heritage was reinforced in my education from elementary to graduate school, as I was taught by members of three religious orders especially devoted to teaching. I recall the Dominican nuns at St. Anthony's sharing stories about learned saints whose feast days we would celebrate. Later, from the Jesuits and Holy Cross priests, I experienced first-hand what Edith Stein is said to have learned from her encounter with Aquinas, namely, that intellectual work can be a service to God. This truth is at the heart of the vocation that has taken shape in me from childhood to the present. I perceive it as a calling to learn and teach and write in light of the Gospel and to do so as part of a mysteriously living communion of Christian teachers and scholars that transcends time and space, united all by a dedication to the life of faith and learning.

Liberal Learning and the Light of Faith: An Initiation into Wholeness

What is it about the life of faith and learning that makes it so compelling, that has drawn the greatest lights of the Church into its service? Its appeal, I think, lies in its promise of an integrated life, that is to say a life that faithfully responds to Christ's command to love God with our heart, soul, and mind. This integration, it seems to me, is the essential task of every Christian educator, but it is not easy, especially at a time when the culture and the academy are inhospitable to it. And yet Christians are still called to serve the Lord in this context, bringing the Good News to the groves of academe.

When I survey the scene in higher education and consider the role that Christians are to play in it, I immediately turn to my intellectual heroes for wisdom. Borrowing the title of Patrick Samway's volume on Walker Percy, let me call these people "signposts in a strange land." Among their number I would include such diverse thinkers as Wendell Berry and John Paul II and Cardinal Newman. The signposts tell us that something is amiss. They alert us to the fact that, yes, we inhabit a strange land. But what makes the land—our land, the land of the academy, not to mention the larger culture—strange? I think that our land is strange because it is too flat; its surface has been reduced, leveled, so that what were once mountains are barely molehills. Or, better, what are mountains are now *reckoned* as molehills. We've got a topographical map that's askew.

Why? Well, if Wendell Berry is right, and I think he is, we've taken our map from the wrong surveyors. The academy's most illustrious mapmakers are reductionists; their equipment is suited to studying small bits of earth, but they presume to measure the whole world with it, to compass the horizon using a microscopic lens. Chief among misguided mapmakers, for Wendell Berry, is Harvard sociobiologist E. O. Wilson. Wilson is a very clever scientist; this Berry grants. But he is a poor philosopher, theologian, and political theorist. Does Wilson claim these areas of expertise? Not exactly. But he presumes to speak on all of them because his method is imperialistic: it conquers every territory of knowledge and becomes its master. In Wilson's own words, "all tangible phenomena, from the birth of stars to the workings of social institutions, are based on material processes that are ultimately reducible to . . . the laws of physics."[2]

That matter is subject to the laws of physics is not the problem.

---

[2] E.O. Wilson, *Consilience* (New York: Knopf, 1998) 266, quoted in Wendell Berry, *Life is a Miracle: An Essay Against Modern Superstition* (Washington, DC: Counterpoint, 2000) 25.

What Wendell Berry and I both object to is the notion that everything tangible is reducible to and, as Wilson argues, determined by the laws of physics. This reductionism is thoroughgoing; there is no room here for a non-material explanation of anything in our experience. Even meaning itself succumbs to the cold clutches of scientific reduction. In Wilson's revealing words, "What we call *meaning* is the linkage among the neural networks created by the spreading excitation that enlarges imagery and engages emotion."[3] Wendell Berry rightly points out that "[t]his idea is explicitly imperialistic, and it is implicitly tyrannical. Mr. Wilson is perfectly frank about his territorial ambitions. He wishes to see all the disciplines linked or unified—but strictly on the basis of science."[4] With meaning reduced to molecules, the profoundest insights of all the disciplines are imperiled. Contrasting the world of Shakespeare's *King Lear* with Wilson's laboratory, Berry notes that only in the former is there a genuine place for the miraculous and mysterious.

But then how has Wilson been able to concoct such a scheme? What has happened here? For Berry, the fact that Wilson can seriously propound the theory of consilience and the fact that he has been richly rewarded for it with accolades and a prestigious post in the academy testifies to the fact that the university has been lost. It is no longer united in any meaningful way, but is fragmented, split into different territories that speak hyper-specialized languages. As Berry argues in "The Loss of the University," there is no common tongue with which to communicate and no forum within which to discuss—and defend—one's ideas.[5] Thus safely distant from theologians and Christian literary scholars, an E. O. Wilson can say that Milton's own testimony notwithstanding, *Paradise Lost* owes nothing to God's inspiration. Without challenge, Wilson is allowed to rest in what E. F. Schumacher called "a methodical aversion to the recognition of higher levels... of significance."[6]

Now this is not a problem in the natural sciences alone; so many of

[3] Wilson, *Consilience*, 115, quoted in Berry, *Life is a Miracle*, 30.

[4] Berry, *Life is a Miracle*, 31.

[5] Wendell Berry, "The Loss of the University," in *Home Economics* (New York: North Point, 1987) 76-97.

[6] E. F. Schumacher, *A Guide for the Perplexed* (New York: Harper & Row, 1978), 43.

our disciplines fall prey to a similar reductionism. This is the predicament of the modern university. But it was not always so; the radical fragmentation of knowledge is a relatively recent thing. As H. J. Massingham has observed, "Modern knowledge is departmentalized," whereas, by contrast, "the essence of culture is *initiation into wholeness*, so that all the divisions of knowledge are considered as the branches of one tree, the Tree of Life whose roots go deep into the earth and whose top is in heaven."[7] Massingham's metaphor signals an alternative vision of learning, one that is worth recovering. This vision is guided by what the medievals called *adaequatio rei et intellectus*: the principle that the understanding of the knower must be adequate to the thing to be known. To put it simply, there are different ways to know different things; and there are different ways to know the same things. Take a book. Let's say the Bible, a first-edition King James at that. Now, a physicist can tell us a great deal about the atomic particles of its parchment; a chemist about the carbon remaining in its pages; a linguist about its distinctive verbal forms; a religious historian about the social and political context of its creation. Yet none of these specialists has comprehended its meaning; each has added to our understanding, yes, but the proper bounds of the disciplines render all of these approaches inadequate to the full reality of the object.

This is why we have universities, optimally communities of learners who complement one another's work in an effort to understand the whole. The recovery of the liberal arts taking place in many of our Christian colleges and universities is a step in the right direction. Even in secular universities, the study of the liberal arts promises some protection against reductionism. To put it positively, the liberal arts in and of themselves can begin one's initiation into wholeness.

Consider this scenario. A non-believing student with an empirical, pragmatic bent enrolls in a state university. He declares a chemistry-major, loads up on natural science courses, and quickly refines his grasp and practice of the scientific method; its precision profoundly shapes his habit of mind. Flush with his newfound knowledge, he examines everything— even his girlfriend—according to its chemical components. (This, of

---

[7] Berry, "Loss of the University," 82. Emphasis added.

course, gets him in trouble.) But in the following semester, he begins to square away his general-education requirements and takes courses on British literature, Western civilization, and art history. Suddenly, he's taken aback. The tools that had served him so well in the lab offer little assistance in interpreting George Herbert or understanding Augustine's *Confessions* or accounting for the paintings of Giotto. Herbert has evoked in him a fascination with language—with the way in which finite forms gesture toward transcendence. Augustine has prompted a new and strange self-examination. Giotto has whetted his appetite for beauty. All of this is mysterious to him, and he can't reduce it to the proportions of chemistry. He has experienced intimations of something beyond. And, like the unforgettable Binx Bolling in Walker Percy's *The Moviegoer*, he undertakes a *search*; he has begun the initiation into wholeness.

What may deliver him into a fuller wholeness? The light of faith. It is the leaven that his studies in the liberal arts need in order to rise to new heights, because a Christian perspective markedly changes the learning process. In what way does it change it? What does it mean to view education, and specifically higher education, from a distinctly Christian perspective? I think it entails at least two things: a certain orientation toward learning and a sense of the proper breadth of education.

CHRISTIAN ORIENTATION TOWARD LEARNING

A Christian orientation toward learning, as I see it, is an openness to the truth that is marked by wonder and gratitude. James Taylor in his remarkable book *Poetic Knowledge: The Recovery of Education* describes wonder as "an emotion of fear, a fear produced by the consciousness of ignorance, which, because it is man's natural desire (good) to know. . . is perceived as a kind of evil,"[8] by which he means a kind of deprivation. Think about the experience of walking into a great study filled from floor to ceiling with beautiful books and at once feeling surges of anxiety and excitement and desire. We are aware that we don't know the riches those books contain; we're daunted by this fact, and yet we're drawn to them just the same; we want to know. As Taylor reckons, this is what Plato and

---

[8] James S. Taylor, *Poetic Knowledge: The Recovery of Education* (Albany: State University of New York Press, 1998) 25.

Aristotle understood as wonder, *the* existential starting point of philosophy.

Plato and Aristotle illuminated much about the experience of wonder and the birth of philosophy in the soul; they were great teachers. But it seems to me that what we learn from Revelation adds immeasurably to our orientation toward learning, because we know from God's self-disclosure to the Jews and, even more, from his Incarnation in Christ that the unmoved mover of the ancients is actually a personal God—so personal that we call him Father—who created the world out of generosity, who considered his creation very good, and who so loved the world even after it rebelled that he sent his only Son to die for its salvation. This perspective, I think, prepares us to approach the learning process not only with wonder, but also with profound gratitude. Everything about our Christian story should encourage this, for we see from start to finish that self-giving love is the very ground of existence; it is the deepest truth about the world. It is out of this love that we have been given everything—from the creation of the world to its salvation—as a gift. And the proper way to receive a gift is thankfully. Thus, the Christian can affirm what Socrates expressed so well about education in the *Republic*, namely, that the object of education is to teach us "to love what is beautiful,"[9] to which she will add, "and to be grateful to her heavenly Father for it."

Christian revelation also informs us that the context within which all learning takes place is a great drama. Think about these biblical themes: the way of life versus the way of death; truth in contest with falsehood; the forces of light arrayed against the powers of darkness; heaven and hell. This means that human life is charged with supernatural meaning, meaning that transcends the bounds of time and history. As Pope John Paul II explains in his encyclical *The Gospel of Life*:

> Man is called to a fullness of life which far exceeds the dimensions of his earthly existence, because it consists in sharing the very life of God. The loftiness of this supernatural vocation reveals the *greatness* and the *inestimable value* of human life even in its temporal phase. Life in time, in fact, is the fundamental condition, the initial stage and an integral part of the entire unified process of human existence. It is a process which, unexpectedly and

---

[9] Plato, *Republic*, 403c.

undeservedly, is enlightened by the promise and renewed by the gift of divine life, which will reach its full realization in eternity (cf. *1 John* 3:1-2). At the same time, it is precisely this supernatural calling which highlights the *relative character* of each individual's earthly life. After all, life on earth is not an "ultimate" but a "penultimate" reality; even so, it remains a *sacred reality* entrusted to us, to be preserved with a sense of responsibility and brought to perfection in love and in the gift of ourselves to God and to our brothers and sisters. [10]

If we understand life as a sacred reality, entrusted to us, we will insist that education remain faithful to the supernatural dimensions and destiny of the human person. Our thoughts about education will begin, as Jacques Maritain's did, with a consideration of the essence of man. "Man," in Maritain's words, "is a person, who holds himself in hand by his intelligence and his will. He does not merely exist as a physical being. There is in him a richer and nobler existence; he has spiritual superexistence through knowledge and love." Thus, contra E. O. Wilson, Maritain insists that man "is in some way, a whole, not merely a part; he is a universe unto himself, a microcosm in which the great universe in its entirety can be encompassed through knowledge." But our capacity to know does not exhaust our personhood, so Maritain quickly follows his observations about man as knower with a reflection on man's singular capacity to love. It is "through love [that] he can give himself freely to beings who are to him, as it were, other selves; and for this relationship no equivalent can be found in the physical world." [11]

A SENSE OF THE BREADTH OF EDUCATION

Man is in some way a whole, a universe unto himself, and education should be commensurate to his stature; this is the second insight a Christian perspective offers. Education must reflect the height, depth, and breadth of human experience, attending to the body, soul, and spirit, to time and eternity. It must, in short, guard against reductionism.

Few have argued as ably as John Henry Newman against this danger, and I think that Christian educators today would do well to revisit his

---

[10] *The Gospel of Life*, n. 2.

[11] Jacques Maritain, *Education at the Crossroads* (New Haven: Yale University Press, 1943) 7-8.

arguments. In important respects, Newman's situation was not unlike our own; he was confronting emergent trends that have now come to fruition, particularly the twin impulses of utilitarian specialization and secularization. Thus the burden of his *Idea of a University* is not only to defend the value of a liberal education against the pragmatic calculus but also to defend the place of theology in the university curriculum. Liberal education, Newman insisted, is a good in itself (since knowledge is a good in itself), though it also has secondary benefits. A cultivated, enlarged, disciplined mind will be useful in any undertaking—social, political, economic, and so forth. And a liberal education must include theological studies, for theological inquiry offers its own, irreplaceable contribution to the common stock of knowledge. Both of these elements strike me as critical to the enterprise of Christian higher education.

From this perspective, then, the university should not attempt to understand the human experience according to the epistemological constraints of any one discipline, nor should it focus on a limited goal, such as career preparation. Instead, as Wendell Berry has insisted, higher education should be about "the making of a good—that is, a fully developed—human being."[12] it would do so by engaging the student in broad, basic studies that enable him to understand the whole, the cosmos. A curriculum should be faithful to the multi-faceted nature of reality, from sub-atomic particles to the heights of religious mysticism, as all reality bears the stamp of God's creative love. In the words of Newman, "All that is good, all that is true, all that is beautiful, all that is beneficent, be it great or small, be it perfect or fragmentary, natural as well as supernatural, moral as well as material, comes from Him."[13]

In short, there should be a Christian impulse to build an expansive, unified curriculum, grounded in the conviction that approaching life and learning through a dedication to the liberal arts illumined by faith provides the surest initiation into wholeness.

---

[12] Berry, "The Loss of the University," 70.
[13] John Henry Newman, *The Idea of a University* (Notre Dame: University of Notre Dame Press, 1982) 50.

SEEING THINGS WHOLE IN THE CLASSROOM

This holistic vision of education cannot be achieved if it remains the work of administrators and curriculum committees; somehow the animating spirit of the whole must be found in each of its parts. This is to say that the integration of faith and learning in the classroom is a critically important enterprise. I think it is critical since genuine Christian faith permeates the whole life of the believer at work, at play, when busy, when at rest, in high celebration and in ordinary time. To be a Christian is an identity, not a role, so it will affect our professional lives as teachers; our most basic commitments permeate all we do. If they did not, our lives would be disastrously bifurcated; what we *do* would be cut off from who we *are*. The attempt to integrate faith and learning in the classroom guards against this division. Or, to state it positively, it affords us the opportunity to live as whole, integrated people whose academic work has something to do with our love of God. What does this mean in practice? I would like to mention four things that it has meant to me, and as I discuss them, I am mindful of the fact that each of these implications will take on a different shape or aspect, depending upon our discipline, temperament, and classroom setting.

The first implication of the argument sketched above is this: To integrate faith and learning in the classroom means that I must be a person of both faith and learning. Underlying this notion is the belief that faith and learning work together: The light of faith illumines the intellect and the cultivated mind penetrates more deeply into faith. As a Christian teacher, I have found that the more I cultivate the spiritual life, the more open I am to the wisdom of my discipline and to sharing that wisdom with my students; likewise, the more faithful I am to my scholarly work, the richer my appreciation of God's purposes in the world. This connection makes sense, given that Jesus reveals himself to be "the way and the truth and the life."[14] This suggests that Truth is personal, not simply propositional and that if I am more deeply connected to the personal source of truth, I will more likely be a better seeker and communicator about truth in all its dimensions. This also suggests that my truth-seeking

---

[14] John 14:6.

has to be informed by a distinctive moral disposition, carefully attuned to the subtle temptations of the academic world. On my best days, I want to imitate Newman, aspiring to live out his authentic Judeo-Christian humanism—what one commentator has described as "a union of intellectual curiosity and achievement with the humility and charity of the truly religious man."[15]

The second practical implication is that I seek to incorporate faith into the course material. In this I am blessed to work at an institution that not only allows but also encourages such integration. This approach includes for me broadening the scope of questions raised and the range of resources drawn upon in addressing the subject matter of the course. I will pose theologically informed questions to my students and will expose them to the insights of Christian intellectual traditions. As a teacher of political theory, I integrate faith and learning by challenging students to penetrate the heart of a thinker's anthropology and by inviting them to assess its adequacy in light of religious wisdom. Bringing the theological perspective into play expands the parameters of the discussion in fruitful ways. For instance, after reading Aristotle's very compelling account of happiness in Book I of the *Ethics*, I present a quite different view taken from the reflections of an American Jesuit missionary to Russia, Walter Ciszek, who had spent over twenty years in Soviet prison on account of his convictions. Whereas Aristotle argues that happiness requires certain external goods, like freedom and health, Ciszek, writing as a former prisoner subject to constant deprivation, provocatively asserts:

> This simple truth, that the sole purpose of man's life on earth is to do the will of God, contains in it riches and resources enough for a lifetime. [...] In this subtle insight of the soul touched by God's divine power lies the root of true interior joy. And as long as this vision persists, as long as the soul does not lose sight of this great truth, the inner joy and peace that follow upon it persist through even the saddest and gravest moments of human trial and suffering. Pain and suffering do not thereby cease to exist; the ache and anguish of body and soul do not vanish from man's consciousness. But even they become a means of nourishing this joy, of

---

[15] Martin Svaglic, introduction to *The Idea of a University* (Notre Dame: University of Notre Dame Press, 1982) xxii.

fostering peace and conformity to God's will, for they are seen as a continuation of Christ's passion.... 16

As the students and I puzzle over the two accounts, I realize time and again that incorporating a distinctly Christian perspective into the discussion leavens the loaf, making it rise to higher dimensions "the dimensions of the soul, suffering, and eternal life" that would not have been reached otherwise. Having spent time in Washington, D.C., in the policy world, I am increasingly persuaded that bringing in this theological perspective is critical for equipping students to engage the most serious political issues facing our polity. One cannot, it seems to me, adequately address such things as abortion or stem-cell research or marriage law without a robust ontology. And I think that religious wisdom alone provides such an ontology.

The third implication I take from the principles sketched above is that as a Christian teacher, I need to pray for my students. Now, praying for my students is not a practice I have perfected by any means, but I think it is worthwhile. In those times when I do pray for my students, I approach the enterprise differently; the difference is subtle but real. I find that when I pray for my students, I am humanized by it, freed just a bit from what is for me *the* occupational hazard of teaching: egotism. I am better able to view the task as subject-centered, not self- centered, and I measure the effectiveness of classroom time less by the positive or negative personal reaction of the students and more according to how well they appropriated the material. Not only does praying for my students humanize me, it humanizes them in my eyes. I perceive their dignity more clearly and am less apt to instrumentalize them. I am better able to live out the wisdom of Jacques Maritain when he says in connection with the instruction of children that:

> [W]hat is of most importance in educators themselves is a respect for the soul as well as for the body of the child, the sense of his innermost essence and his internal resources, and a sort of sacred and loving attention to his mysterious identity, which is a hidden thing that no techniques can reach.[17]

---

[16] Walter J. Ciszek, S. J., *He Leadeth Me* (San Francisco: Ignatius Press, 1995) 117-18.

[17] Maritain, 9.

In short, it is when I pray for my students that I am able to see my profession as a vocation, as a high calling to serve the sacred reality of my students.

Finally, I have found that integrating faith and learning in the classroom is assisted by not only praying *for* the students, but *with* them. Teaching at a university like Villanova makes this possible. Following the lead of several of my mentors at Notre Dame, I begin each class with a brief prayer and invite the students to join me if they wish. To paraphrase St. Paul, one might say that the classroom "is made holy by the invocation of God in prayer."[18] I have come to view this as a privilege and a blessing, and it's a practice that has been well received by the students. In praying before class I find that in a very concrete way I integrate my professional role and my Christian identity, while connecting academic work with the love of God. Placing our common work in the context of prayer is to remind us of the only context that gives our studies their full meaning.

CONCLUSION

To approach education in its fullest context is the unique privilege and responsibility of the Christian educator. Confident that the Gospel illuminates the whole of reality, she has the opportunity to enrich the liberal arts with the light of faith, drawing out the depth, breadth, height, and hue of every inquiry. Unlike her secular colleagues, the Christian professor provides a window onto a technicolored and richly textured world of divine purpose. Inviting students into this world, she introduces them to "the dramatic structure of truth"[19] within which learning takes place. And by making this introduction, she offers her students an initiation into wholeness—a wholeness that is the very substance of the teaching vocation.

---

[18] 1 Timothy 4:4-5.

[19] David C. Schindler, *Hans Urs von Balthasar and the Dramatic Structure of Truth: A Philosophical Investigation* (New York: Fordham University Press, 2004).

CHAPTER TEN

Where Are the Baptists in the Higher Education Dialogue?

William E. Hull
Samford University

Ours is a time, perhaps as never before, when Baptist higher education needs to be at its best: united in spirit, shrewd in strategy, competitive in attracting resources, compelling in its case for an educational experience with a robust religious component. But when we take soundings of the contemporary situation, our findings leave much to be desired. At crucial points the enterprise is divided in spirit, confused in strategy, declining in constituency support, and unable to articulate with any urgency either the need for, or the distinctiveness of, education rooted in a Baptist ethos. Why is this the case?

I.

The dramatic redirection of the Southern Baptist Convention (SBC) over the past quarter-century (1979-2004) is a well-known story that need not be repeated here.[1] But the consequences of this self-styled "conservative

---

[1] The literature is voluminous. A few of the sources relevant to this inquiry include Bill J. Leonard, *God's Last and Only Hope: The Fragmentation of the Southern Baptist Convention* (Grand Rapids: Eerdmans, 1990); Walter B. Shurden, editor, *The Struggle for the Soul of the SBC: Moderate Responses to the Fundamentalist Movement* (Macon, GA: Mercer University Press, 1993); Nancy Tatum Ammerman, editor, *Southern Baptists Observed: Multiple Perspectives on a Changing Denomination* (Knoxville: University of Tennessee Press, 1993); David T. Morgan, *The New Crusades, The New Holy Land: Conflict in the Southern Baptist Convention, 1969-1991* (Tuscaloosa, AL: University of Alabama Press, 1996); Barry Hankins, *Uneasy in*

resurgence" continue to exert an impact on the higher-education enterprise.[2] By voting to abolish the SBC Education Commission in 1996, the denomination announced its intention to pursue a national strategy in which liberal-arts education played no part (except in a few Bible colleges developed as appendages to its seminaries). Consistent with this decision, stress on education has simply disappeared from the SBC agenda. For example, the latest comprehensive campaign, called "Empowering Kingdom Growth," has "seven pillars" or foundational emphases, none of which even remotely relates to the life of the mind.

A good way to monitor such trends is through Baptist Press, which daily reports in some detail what denominational leaders want the public to know about the character of Baptist life. It is striking to observe how less and less attention is being devoted to intellectual issues while more and more attention is being paid to advocacy issues involving the federal government. Clearly the gatekeepers of Baptist news believe that partisan politics is a far more important instrument than academic inquiry in achieving their goals.

Even though Baptist colleges and universities have always been sponsored at the state level, I began with a comment on the national convention because a relentless effort is being made to push the mindset and approach of the SBC into each of the cooperating state conventions, district associations, and local churches. Even though each of these levels of denominational life is theoretically autonomous according to Baptist polity, a long history of voluntary connectionalism between these several entities makes top-down pressure from the SBC both powerful and pervasive. To be sure, well-established educational institutions have more loyal supporters in their home state than elsewhere, which tends to protect them from the kind of forced takeovers that traumatized the SBC seminaries in the 1990s. But strong-willed leaders who led insurgency at the national level almost invariably display the same instincts closer to home.

Babylon: Southern Baptist Conservatives and American Culture (Tuscaloosa, AL: University of Alabama Press, 2002).

[2] For a more detailed history of the impact of this denominational controversy on higher education see William E. Hull, *Southern Baptist Higher Education: Retrospect and Prospect* (Birmingham: Samford University, 2001).

The resulting destabilization may be illustrated by a quick survey of the present situation.[3] Early on in the 1980s and 1990s, four of our most historic schools severed all ties with their state convention: Richmond, Wake Forest, Furman, and Stetson. They were soon followed by Meredith and Grand Canyon; then by Missouri Baptist and Shorter, whose separations are being bitterly contested in the courts; and most recently by William Jewell. In addition to these outright divorces, an almost equal number of schools have sought to gain greater control of their governance structure, a move that could be viewed as a distancing from denominational sponsorship at the point of trustee selection: Baylor, Carson-Newman, Houston Baptist, Mississippi College, Ouachita, Palm Beach Atlantic, and Samford. Beyond this, yet other schools are currently in open conflict with various elements of their Baptist constituency in ways that could lead to further ruptures, especially Averett, Louisiana College, and Mars Hill.

What does it mean for nineteen out of fifty-four colleges and universities to go through wrenching upheaval in little more than a decade? In almost every instance the changes were contentious, often engulfing the campus in controversy for months if not years. In most cases, opposition arose, not over principled objection to educational policy, but as a naked struggle for institutional control. The result was that conflict could strike anytime or anywhere, leaving schools vulnerable to the vicissitudes of denominational politics. In response to such threats, a number of presidents were forced to recommend a drastic course of action that could have cost them their job if not accepted. Despite these formidable challenges, courageous leaders kept their poise and refused to allow a siege mentality to settle on their campuses.

Nevertheless, the consequences of this internecine strife have been significant: everyone involved was distracted from addressing the primary agenda of education, a cautionary attitude stifled bold innovation, and living defensively led to a loss of momentum in claiming the promise of a new millennium. This situation does much to explain the muting of a Baptist voice in the higher-education dialogue. Two illustrations will suffice. First,

---

[3] For a brief overview, with particular attention to the trials of Shorter College, see Beth McMurtrie, "Religion and Politics," *Chronicle of Higher Education* (July 4, 2003): A20-A22.

since 1972, the H. I. Hester Lectures have provided a primary forum for Baptist leaders to grapple seriously with issues confronting Christian higher education. In a pre-controversy collection of outstanding contributions to this series, the majority of the authors were Baptist, whereas in a post-controversy collection only three authors were Baptist, two of them repeats from the earlier volume and none of them with a long-term connection to a Southern Baptist-related school.[4] Second, *Christian Scholar's Review* regularly carries announcements of major national conferences on some aspect of Christian higher education. The four most recent conferences feature twenty-six plenary speakers, only two of them Baptist, one from Canada and the other from Nigeria.[5]

What these two illustrations suggest is that when Baptist educators gather to think about their task they tend to listen to others, yet when non-Baptist educators gather to do the same they tend not to listen to Baptists, especially from Southern Baptist ranks. This observation is not offered as a criticism of our institutions for lacking star speakers who can command the ear of the academic world. Rather it is a lament that many of our brightest minds have been so distracted by denominational controversy that they have not been able to develop their great gifts in a

---

[4] The earlier volume edited by Arthur L. Walker, Jr., *Integrating Faith and Academic Discipline: Selected H. I. Hester Lectures* (Nashville: Education Commission of the Southern Baptist Convention, 1992) includes contributions by twelve authors, seven of them Baptist. The later volume edited by Douglas V. Henry and Bob R. Agee, *Faithful Learning and the Christian Scholarly Vocation* (Grand Rapids: Eerdmans, 2003) has nine contributors, the three Baptists being Anthony Campolo and Denton Lotz from the previous volume, both with American Baptist backgrounds, and Stephen Evans who only recently joined the Baylor faculty after serving at Wheaton, St. Olaf, and Calvin.

[5] The four conferences being advertized as this was written were on "Christianity & the Soul of the University" by the Council of Christian Scholarly Societies, March 25-27, 2004, with four plenary speakers; "Slavery, Oppression, and Prejudice" by the Baylor Institute for Faith and Learning, September 30-October 2, 2004, with six plenary speakers; "Faith in the Academy" by Messiah College, September 30-October 2, 2004, with eleven plenary speakers; and "Christian Faith and the Historian's Vocation" by The Conference on Faith and History, October 14-16, 2004, with five plenary speakers (later reduced to three plenary speakers on the Web site). The two Baptists among the twenty-six are the Canadian David Jeffrey, now at Baylor University, and the Nigerian Caleb Oladipo, now at Baptist Theological Seminary in Richmond.

climate conducive to creativity. To revert to the assigned title of this essay, my first answer to the question, "Where are the Baptists in the higher education dialogue?," would be: They are hunkered down doing good work while valiantly trying to survive! Sad to report, Baptist educators are not saying much of anything either to themselves or to others because they have not had the encouragement of their denominational constituency to develop a grand new vision of what Christian higher education with a Baptist ethos might mean for the twenty-first century.

The lack of such a shared vision uniting church and school is best seen in the way that the two Southern Baptist schools most aggressively seeking to innovate have done so by adopting models not indigenous to the Baptist educational experience. I refer to Union University, which is adapting approaches characteristic of those schools that are sponsored by evangelical groups, and to Baylor University, which is "embracing" number of emphases that are found in schools sponsored by denominations with traditions rooted in the established churches of Europe. Both of these options in higher education are manifesting a good bit of energy today, hence it is not surprising that two of our institutions would turn to them for fresh impetus at a time when Baptist thinking is suffering from battle fatigue. We now take a closer look at the strategies of these two schools.

II.

Union University, under the leadership of David S. Dockery, its current president since 1995, has become a textbook case of how a Baptist-related school may utilize the evangelical paradigm in its approach to Christian higher education. In terms of the context sketched above, this experiment is of particular interest because it seeks to transcend and thereby reconcile the enormous tensions provoked by recent denominational realignments. Located in West Tennessee, one of the more conservative regions of the Convention, called Landmark Country by those who know the history, Union has reached outside Southern Baptist life for a new model in the hope of serving all sides of a divided denominational constituency.

Evidence of the evangelical pattern abounds at Union.[6] Key

---

[6] The examples cited here are taken primarily from its Web site (www.uu.edu)

statements of purpose and mission focus on "thinking Christianly," on "the integration of faith and learning," and on looking at life "through the lenses of a Christian worldview." Prominent on the Web site is a lengthy bibliography dominated by evangelical books that address these specific concerns. Seven centers have been established to help the different departments "deal Christianly" with their disciplines, plus a Baconian Society that fosters "the science-faith dialogue." Evangelical icons such as Carl F. H. Henry and Charles Colson are evoked in the naming of key centers and professorships. The roster of recent speakers is a Who's Who of the evangelical world: Joel Carpenter, Duane Litfin, Os Guinness, Michael Behe, and Harry Stout. Likewise, recent Scholars-in-Residence include such evangelical worthies as Arthur Holmes, Anthony Thiselton, and James Sire. While there is certainly no effort to disguise its denominational rootage and affiliation, the Union of today would be instantly recognizable as one of their own by evangelicals who know nothing of Southern Baptist life.

In evaluating this strategy, the adoption of an evangelical paradigm certainly has much to commend it.[7] In many ways, Evangelicalism is the great religious success story of the second half of the twentieth century, particularly in guiding a broad populist movement prone to controversy from the obscurantism of a fundamentalist past to cultural legitimacy in the academic world. Think of the amazing evolution of Billy Graham's career from tent revivalist to world statesman.[8] Or of Fuller Seminary's

---

and from its Provost Report for 2003. For more detail see the Union contributors to David S. Dockery and David P. Gushee, editors, *The Future of Christian Higher Education* (Nashville: Broadman & Holman, 1999); David S. Dockery and Gregory Alan Thornbury, *Shaping a Christian Worldview: The Foundations of Christian Higher Education* (Nashville: Broadman & Holman, 2002).

[7] A good summary of evangelical strengths in higher education is provided by Mark A. Noll in the first of his 2003 Hester Lectures, "Christian Thinking in 2003 America," *The Educator* (Third Quarter, 2003): 3-8; and by D. G. Hart, *That Old-Time Religion in Modern America: Evangelical Protestantism in the Twentieth Century* (Chicago: Ivan R. Dee, 2002) 115-43. For a sympathetic audit by an outsider see Alan Wolfe, "The Opening of the Evangelical Mind," *The Atlantic Monthly* (October, 2000): 55-76.

[8] The move of Graham from the margins to the mainstream of American culture is a favorite theme of Marshal Frady, *Billy Graham: A Parable of American Righteousness* (Boston: Little, Brown, 1979).

journey from ambiguous beginnings to a pacesetting role in theological education.[9] Or, of the growth of *Christianity Today* from a struggling fortnightly to a journalistic empire with *Books & Culture* as its sophisticated showcase.[10] In the academic arena, can Southern Baptist colleges and universities match the intellectual resources of Calvin and Wheaton? Do we have historians the equal of George Marsden and Mark Noll, or philosophers of the stature of Alvin Plantinga and Nicholas Wolterstorff? Are we supported by publishers with backlists as rich as Eerdmans and Baker/Brazos? Or by foundations as generous as the Lilly Endowment and the Pew Charitable Trusts?

Although there is a lot to like about evangelical higher education, any Baptist school evaluating this option would need to consider its downside. To begin with, Baptist higher education has long been denominational, characterized by strong patterns of connectionalism designed to serve a diverse historical movement. By contrast, evangelical higher education is mainly inter-denominational or non-denominational, reflecting a fluid confederation of groupings that shows a remarkable ability to shift in ways that take even its own adherents by surprise. Lacking a strong doctrine of the church, Evangelicalism has characteristically used confessional fidelity to define and maintain its fragile unity, but these statements of faith are often so tightly drawn that they reflect the beliefs of only about twenty percent of the American population and an even smaller percentage of the American professoriate. While this selective pool might suffice for a single school of national reputation such as Calvin or Wheaton, it is much harder to contemplate staffing the 8,000 faculty and administrative positions in fifty Southern Baptist schools when the bar is set to exclude not only Catholics and Jews but a host of mainline Protestant academics as well.

When it comes to fulfilling educational responsibilities, no one has

---

[9] An important history of the tortured transformation of Fuller Seminary is George M. Marsden, *Reforming Fundamentalism: Fuller Seminary and the New Evangelicalism* (Grand Rapids: Eerdmans, 1987).

[10] For insight into the strategy lying behind *Books & Culture* see the undated and unpublished Prospectus prepared by Mark A. Noll, "An Evangelical Review?" Important to the originating ferment was a lengthy essay by Nathan O. Hatch and Michael S. Hamilton, "Can Evangelicalism Survive Its Success?" *Christianity Today* (October 5, 1992): 20-31.

been harder on evangelicals than their own premier historian, Mark Noll. Writing the introductory volume to a comprehensive history of the movement, he remarks on the "oddity that the greatest intellectual in the whole history of evangelicalism was also its first great intellectual,"[11] Jonathan Edwards, who flourished 1730-57. Before the eighteenth century was over, it was clear that Evangelicalism would be a people-oriented renewal movement strong on personal piety and practical wisdom but weak on foundational reasoning and comprehensive analysis. In a stinging critique of its contemporary condition, called *The Scandal of the Evangelical Mind*, Noll lamented the disastrous effects of nineteenth- and twentieth-century fundamentalism, revivalism, pragmatism, and dispensationalism in building a credible intellectual culture.[12] Even with full appreciation for the many achievements summarized above, the latest verdict of the man who knows Evangelicalism best from the inside is sobering indeed:

> Problems remain concerning the ability to sustain intellectual vigor in an environment in which evangelical subcultures easily run off into escapist literature (especially novels about the return of Christ), political extremism (usually of the Right), polemical science (especially scientific creationism), and affective anti-intellectualism (especially in some of the modern praise songs).[13]

In asking how the evangelical paradigm might actually work in a Baptist context, we turn to the 2004 Hester Lecture by David Dockery, which is the latest and presumably most mature rationale for the effort at Union by its acknowledged leader.[14] Here the central focus is on the need

---

[11] Mark A. Noll, *The Rise of Evangelicalism: The Age of Edwards, Whitefield and the Wesleys*, vol. 1, *A History of Evangelicalism: People, Movements and Ideas in the English-Speaking World* (Downers Grove, IL: InterVarsity, 2003), 256.

[12] Mark A. Noll, *The Scandal of the Evangelical Mind* (Grand Rapids: Eerdmans, 1994).

[13] Mark A. Noll, "Foreward: American Past and World Present in the Search for Evangelical Identity," *Pilgrims on the Sawdust Trail: Evangelical Ecumenism and the Quest for Christian Identity*, edited by Timothy George. Beeson Divinity Studies (Grand Rapids: Baker Academic, 2004), 17.

[14] David S. Dockery, "Toward a Theology of/for Baptist Higher Education," Hester Lecture to the Association of Southern Baptist Colleges and Schools, June 1, 2004, unpublished manuscript scheduled for publication in *The Educator*. Hereinafter cited without title as Dockery.

WILLIAM E. HULL   133

for "an explicit theology of and for Baptist higher education rooted in the imperatives of the Christian gospel."[15] Such "a distinctive Baptist theology will have Christ at its center, the church as its focus, and the influencing of culture as a key element of its vision."[16] Again, it will "cultivate a holistic orthodoxy, based on a high view of scripture and congruent with the Trinitarian and Christological consensus of the early church."[17]

As Dockery develops this emphasis he seems to end up with a variant of the "two-spheres" approach. In one sphere is a "bedrock, non-negotiable commitment" to "an ancient kind of orthodoxy, a primitive but passionate core of theological truths" not unlike the classic creeds.[18] In the other sphere is "our love for study... the place of research... the significance of honest exploration, reflection, and intellectual wrestling... new discovery and creative teaching."[19] And what is to be the relationship between these two spheres, "the Christian tradition" on one side and "honest intellectual inquiry" on the other?[20] The operative word appears to be "tension," further described as co-existence "in an enriching dialectical dependence."[21] The conclusion seems inescapable: since higher education has always emphasized a head full of information and ideas, and since Christianity has always emphasized a heart full of faith and love, therefore Christian higher education must emphasize a combination of the two.

At first glance, this approach may seem to reflect a tradeoff according to which educators are being told: "In exchange for adherence to the highest claims of canon and creed so as to satisfy the needs of your supporting constituency, you are free to explore the frontiers of knowledge so as to satisfy the needs of your brightest students." Nor can it be denied that some of the most vociferous critics of Baptist higher education are often heard to say, "Don't bother me with your scholarly theories; I just

---

[16] Dockery, 3.
[17] Dockery, 9.
[18]Dockery, 28-29.
[19] Dockery, 26.
[20] Dockery, 21.
[21] Dockery, 21.

want to know if you believe what I do!" But viewing the "two-spheres" approach in this fashion does not go far enough because Dockery, true to his evangelical paradigm, is insistent that the two spheres be "integrated," which for him "means being able to see life from a Christian vantage point; it means thinking theologically across the curriculum," or, as T. S. Eliot put it, "to think in Christian categories."[22]

But it is just here that a host of key operational questions remain unanswered, three of which may be mentioned. We begin with the superiority issue: in the "tension" that accompanies the integration of faith and knowledge, does theology finally trump the findings of the various disciplines and, if so, why? Have theologians more often been right than historians or scientists or poets? To be sure, theologians deal with the "special revelation" of God's saving story grounded in uniquely inspired Scripture, but did those ancient authors also give us the last word on the many branches of knowledge that the modern university pursues? So, for example, if a conflict arises between a theologian and a physicist regarding the way in which the physical universe is constructed, does the theologian always win? Dockery speaks often of how "theology and tradition" can correct "the directionless state that characterizes so much of higher education today,"[23] but there is no mention of how the findings of higher education ever correct theology and tradition. All I am asking here is whether his approach has adequate built-in safeguards to prevent another Galileo fiasco.

Second, lurking in what seems to be an implicit theological triumphalism is the hermeneutical issue. Dockery clearly wants the consensus theology of our confessional heritage to exercise a normative role in shaping the way that we understand all knowledge. Everywhere he seems to assume that there is a fixity, even a finality, to "the great tradition flowing from the Apostles' Creed to the confessions of Nicea in 325 and Chalcedon in 451."[24] But how are we to interpret this deposit: as it was understood 1,600 years ago or as it would be understood today? Based on the promise that the Holy Spirit will lead us into truth that heretofore we

---

[22] Dockery, 23.
[23] Dockery, 22.
[24] Dockery, 10.

were unable to grasp (John 16:12-13), may we say that our understanding of this ancient legacy not only *will* change but *should* change as God gives us new knowledge and deeper insight? The hermeneutical task is a two-way street from which canon and creed are not exempt. Even though their content never changes, just as the Shakespearian corpus never changes, *our understanding* of their content constantly changes as we build upon the past and develop new modes of thought.

Since hermeneutics is such a complex process, let me offer a specific illustration. Take the two affirmations regarding creation and consummation that bracket the core of the classic creeds. When we ask what it might mean to have a curriculum "framed" by such faith-informed convictions, two interrelated questions immediately arise. When we confess God first as the maker and finally as the remaker of heaven and earth, how shall we utilize the findings of modern science in our quest for understanding? Again, how does the preferred theological tradition help us to answer this inescapable hermeneutical question? Unfortunately, the answer is that contemporary Evangelicalism finds itself in almost complete disarray regarding both protology and eschatology, as may easily be seen from the detailed reports of Ronald Numbers and Paul Boyer.[25] This confusion does not mean that these historic doctrines have lost their credibility, only that our efforts to understand them are often a slow and clumsy process in which we need all the help we can get, including the insights of non-theologians.

Third, this recognition of our mutual interdependence in the quest for truth leads directly to the issue of epistemology. Permeating Dockery's presentation is an assumption common to many evangelicals that theology, particularly when it embraces "a holistic orthodoxy," confers a greater degree of certitude regarding truth than is possible by pursuing any of the other routes to reality being offered by the various academic disciplines. In all that he says about the theological sphere, one searches in vain for any emphasis on either the essential mystery of all that is divine or the essential ignorance of all that is human. Doubt seems to play no positive

---

[25] Ronald L. Numbers, *The Creationists* (New York: Alfred A. Knopf, 1992); Paul Boyer, *When Time Shall Be No More: Prophecy Belief in Modern American Culture* (Cambridge: Belknap Press, 1992).

role in theology's quest for truth, yet doubt regarding the adequacy of received wisdom is the great driver of scholarship's insatiable quest for new discoveries through original research. Why does Evangelicalism find it so hard to confess, especially in an educational context, that we "know in part" (1 Corinthians 13:12) in the face of a *Deus absconditus* (Isaiah 45:15)?

Here, again, a single illustration may suffice. When Evangelicalism was at the peak of its ascendancy in mid-nineteenth-century America, its most intellectual southern advocates insisted with categorical finality that God had instituted slavery in perpetuity as plainly taught by Scripture, the only omnicompetent, infallible authority for life. This position was taken, not in capitulation to cultural pressure, but as the result of a carefully argued theology of hierarchy that some are still using today to subordinate women. Indeed, so certain were southern evangelicals of their transcendent justification of slavery that they branded northern abolitionists as infidels who had abandoned the literal teaching of the Bible for the secular ideology of the Enlightenment.[26] Dockery would undoubtedly repudiate this now-discredited evangelical position, but how does the operation of his model keep this kind of thing from happening today just as it did 150 years ago? All I am pleading for here is more epistemological modesty in asserting the claims of the theologians since their record is hardly unblemished.

I leave it to each reader to decide on the potential of the evangelical paradigm for Baptist higher education, even as I commend Union University and its president for providing us with a clear and comprehensive example of how it might be implemented. For myself, this option remains questionable at best because of the divided mind of the evangelical movement. If it were to tilt toward the vision of a Mark Noll I would be much encouraged, for all that he advocates and personally accomplishes demonstrates what a great contribution Christianity can make to higher education. But if it were to tilt toward the vision of a Tim LaHaye I would be much discouraged because his high-profile contributions continue to

---

[26] The theological position of antebellum southern evangelicals on slavery is well described by Mark A. Noll, "The Bible and Slavery," *Religion and the American Civil War*, edited by Randall M. Miller, Harry S. Stout, and Charles Reagan Wilson (New York: Oxford University Press, 1998), 43-50. Noll expanded his analysis in *America's God: From Jonathan Edwards to Abraham Lincoln* (New York: Oxford University Press, 2002) 365-85.

reflect the scandal of the evangelical mind to those seeking to be intellectually serious. Right now LaHaye is winning the battle at the grassroots level where Evangelicalism really lives.[27] I cannot guess what so unpredictable a movement will next become, which means that only time will tell the enduring value of this paradigm for our Baptist schools.

III.

For those hesitant to embrace Evangelicalism as an escape from the present Baptist malaise, another option now gaining strength is what I shall call the establishment paradigm because it has long been nourished by Roman Catholicism, which invented the modern university, and by its Lutheran and Reformed offsprings. What all three of these traditions share in common is a European rootage where they were established as a state church, the official religion of the realm. For this reason they developed a deep sense of responsibility for the total culture of the people, thereby defining the mission of higher education in comprehensive terms as propagating and preserving what we have come to view as Western civilization.

With the triumph of disestablishmentarianism in America, these churches lost their privileged position in the public square but, at various times and places in our history, they have exercised a cultural hegemony that kept alive the memory of their role in the Old World. This experience shaped a distinctive philosophy of education, especially, in Catholicism, with five characteristics that differ notably from their counterpart in Evangelicalism:

> (1) an emphasis on the continuity of faith and reason, (2) respect for the cumulative wisdom of past generations in the tradition, (3) an effort to be inclusive in membership and values, (4) acknowledgment of the communitarian aspect of the redemption, and (5) the pervasive appreciation of the sacramental principle.[28]

---

[27] Larry Eskridge, "And the Most Influential American Evangelical of the Last 25 Years Is ....," *Institute for the Study of American Evangelicals* 17, no. 4 (2001): 1-4.
[28] Monika K. Hellwig, "What Can the Roman Catholic Tradition Contribute to Christian Higher Education?" *Models for Christian Higher Education: Strategies for*

Baptists wishing to examine the implementation of these principles on a smaller campus might look at St. Olaf and Valparaiso, both Lutheran, or at Calvin as a hybrid of Reformed Evangelicalism and Kuyperian Establishmentarianism. For a look at larger campuses there are a number of major Catholic universities as different as Georgetown, Boston College, Marquette, DePaul, and Loyola of Chicago. But pride of place must go to Notre Dame for a host of reasons. It is securely ensconced in the coveted "top fifty" of National Universities-Doctoral, usually ranked about eighteenth. It is well resourced with a three million-volume library and a three-billion dollar endowment recently enhanced by a $1.1 billion capital campaign. It has over 11,000 students on a 136-building campus with a distinguished faculty offering research doctorates in twenty-two fields, many of primary concern to Christian scholars. Perhaps most important, it has been very intentional in planning careful strategies for the exercise of its impressive stewardship as the most famous Christian university in the world.[29]

Carl Henry used to plead on the pages of *Christianity Today* for evangelicals to do what Catholics have done at Notre Dame, namely, to develop at least one front-rank doctoral university for the training of its future intellectual leadership, all to no avail. But is it thinkable that we could do what evangelicals failed to do and create a Baptist Notre Dame? Now, in Baylor University, we have a contender willing to accept that challenge.[30] Under the leadership of Robert B. Sloan, Jr., president since 1995, it has launched a ten-year strategic plan called "Baylor 2012," which defines the aspirations of the Baptist school in terms reminiscent of the Catholic school.[31] The ambitious 42-page blueprint announces four key

---

Survival and Success in the Twenty-First Century, edited by Richard T. Hughes and William B. Adrian (Grand Rapids: Eerdmans, 1997), 14 (numbering added).

[29] Note especially two unpublished internal reports, "Priorities and Commitments for Excellence," dated November 30, 1982; and "Colloquy for the Year 2000," dated May 7, 1993.

[30] I have not seen in print a claim by Baylor that it is seeking to become a Baptist Notre Dame, anymore than by Union that it is seeking to become a Baptist Wheaton, but the connection is commonplace among observers, e.g. Robert Benne, *Quality with Soul: How Six Premier Colleges and Universities Keep Faith with Their Religious Tradition* (Grand Rapids: Eerdmans, 2001) 112.

[31] "Baylor 2012: Ten Year Vision" as adopted by the Board of Regents on

goals: (1) To move from second tier to first tier as one of the "top fifty" National Universities-Doctoral. (2) To do so by recruiting a world-class faculty skilled in research and graduate education. (3) To become "one of the great Christian universities in the world" that encourages "the integration of Christian faith and the intellectual life" throughout the curriculum. (4) To engage in a massive building program that will make the campus far more residential as a center for enriched community life.

Nor can it be denied that Baylor is the best candidate to become a Baptist Notre Dame, Wake Forest having moved in other directions. Both schools were founded at about the same time, Notre Dame in 1842 and Baylor in 1845. Both are located in small cities, Notre Dame in South Bend, Indiana, and Baylor in Waco, Texas. Both are of similar size, the more selective Notre Dame with 11,500 students, Baylor with 13,500 students. In financial resources and in what they can provide, such as faculty size and physical facilities, Notre Dame is well ahead of Baylor, but Texas offers a fertile field for fund-raising when its economy is flourishing. The biggest gap of all is in prestige, and it is precisely this reputational deficit that "Baylor 2012" seeks to address, even though Notre Dame will prove to be a worthy competitor in the arena of educational elitism because of a fierce "Catholic pride" symbolized by its legendary gridiron prowess.

When we ask whether this establishment paradigm might actually work at a school such as Baylor, or whether the very notion of a Baptist Notre Dame is an oxymoron, at least three issues among many invite our attention. The first concerns the tenacious localism of the Baptist tradition. Like every other Southern Baptist school, Baylor was founded to serve only one region of the country. The official motto inscribed on its seal reflects this deliberate sense of boundedness: *Pro Ecclesia, Pro Texana*. Baylor has always been supported by Texas Baptists. Its regents are Texas Baptists. Its presidents have long been Texas Baptists. Over 10,000 of its students are from Texas, the majority of them Baptist. In recruiting faculty nationally, many of the new hires obviously could not be from Texas, prompting anguished cries from some of the University's "first

---

September 21, 2001, is available from the Office of the President in oversize booklet form with art work and pictures, as well on the Web site www.baylor.edu/vision in a 42-page study edition.

families," whose lineage includes recent presidents, that this new approach was eroding the sense of campus camaraderie rooted in a common Texas heritage.

At the most basic level we may wonder if Texas will ever let Baylor become a truly national university.[32] Remember that the centerpiece of President Hesburgh's strategy at Notre Dame was to laicize and nationalize its board of trustees in 1967.[33] Texas hubris notwithstanding, only a distinguished national board of influential leaders can open doors from coast to coast to the kind of money necessary to fund a pacesetting private university. Historically, Baptist efforts to go national, as in the cases of Columbian University and the University of Chicago, have been singularly unsuccessful because of our decentralized denominational polity.[34] By contrast, Catholic universities have long been part of an international network on which Notre Dame could draw in spreading its reputation far and wide.[35]

A second issue is faculty recruitment, which includes at least two aspects. To begin with, where will Baylor find sufficient Baptist firepower both to publish cutting-edge research in the disciplines and, at the same time, to guide the integration of Christian faith and intellectual life? Assuming an eventual faculty of around 1,000, which is where Notre Dame is today, and a "critical mass" of 50%, we are talking about upwards of 500 people. Having been on the lookout for exactly this kind of person for a great many years, I would wonder if there are as many as fifty in Baptist

---

[32] The issues involved in a Texas institution becoming a national institution have been perceptively analyzed by a leader in the "Baylor 2012" effort, Michael D. Beaty, "Baptist Models: Past, Present, and Future," *The Future of Religious Colleges: The Proceedings of the Harvard Conference on the Future of Religious Colleges, October 6-7, 2000*, edited by Paul J. Dovre (Grand Rapids: Eerdmans, 2002), 136-40.

[33] Theodore M. Hesburgh, *The Hesburgh Papers: Higher Values in Higher Education* (Kansas City: Andrews and McMeel, 1979), 36, 69-71; Theodore M. Hesburgh with Jerry Reedy, *God, Country, Notre Dame* (New York: Doubleday, 1990), 170-88.

[34] For brief comment in a helpful context see William H. Brackney, "Secularization of the Academy: A New Challenge to Baptist Historians," *Baptist History & Heritage* 39, no. 1 (2004): 66.

[35] Hesburgh regularly attended and spoke to the International Association of Universities, a UNESCO-affiliated organization based in Paris. For five years he was president of the International Federation of Catholic Universities, which took him to all parts of the world. See Hesburgh, *The Hesburgh Papers*, 17, 36.

life today? And even if there were, do we want to concentrate most or all of them on one campus? Baylor has begun its new strategy by plucking some of the low-hanging fruit from sister Baptist schools, but the pickings are likely to be pretty slim going forward. Even if the needed core be cut in half to 250, Baylor will have a much harder time finding its critical mass among sixteen million Southern Baptists than Notre Dame did among sixty million Roman Catholics.

A related aspect of this issue is how the new breed of recruits will relate to existing faculty, especially to senior colleagues with tenure. Thus far, the use of generous financial incentives and prestigious titles to lure some of the new cadre has created the suspicion of a "two-tier" faculty, which can prove very adverse to the morale of a professoriate that often cherishes status more than power. Careful surveys of the faculty show that the majority do not put the highest emphasis on research and do not know how to teach their courses from a Christian perspective.[36] Clearly many of them feel that the adoption of "Baylor 2012" suddenly devalued their contribution despite many years of loyal service to the university including active participation in its religious life. This attitude is intensified every time they recommend faculty candidates much like themselves, only to have the administration veto them because they do not fit the guidelines of the new strategic plan. There is a totalist ring to the rhetoric of "Baylor 2012," as if the train is leaving the station and everybody needs to be on board, instead of balancing its distinctive initiatives with a healthy appreciation for diversity lest Baylor become a "Baptist bubble" in which

[36] Survey data indicate that only 35% of the Baylor faculty put the "maximum possible emphasis" on research, as compared to 75% of the Notre Dame faculty. At Baylor, 56% of the faculty claim that they are unable to "create a syllabus for a course they currently teach that includes a clear, academically-legitimate Christian perspective on the subject." Indeed, 74% are not prepared to concede that "considering Christian perspectives more than others in the core curriculum" is one of Baylor's distinctive tasks. For an analysis of these data see Michael Beaty, Todd Buras, and Larry Lyon, "Christian Higher Education: An Historical and Philosophical Perspective," *Perspectives in Religious Studies* 24, no. 2 (1997): 163; Larry Lyon and Michael Beaty, "Integration, Secularization, and the Two-Spheres View at Religious Colleges: Comparing Baylor University with the University of Notre Dame and Georgetown College," *Christian Scholar's Review* 29, no. 1, (1999): 86-89.

only one approach to truth is privileged.[37]

Our third issue is that of curricular content, which is raised by the honest recognition that Baptists have never had a comprehensive theology or philosophy of any kind. Our denominational thinkers have been pastor-theologians and seminary teachers concerned primarily with an understanding of conversion and church life.[38] There is simply no Baptist position, or even a body of Baptist thought, on most of the areas addressed by Baylor's curriculum except for a few religion courses. As Mark Noll put it to us plainly: "When studying Baptist history, it is difficult to discern a distinctly Baptist contribution to the life of the mind." For example, "there has never been, to my knowledge, a Baptist metaphysic, a Baptist art history, a Baptist epistemology, a Baptist interpretation of the Thirty Years War, and so forth." The themes that do recur, such as localism, populism, and voluntarism, "often coexist with a lack of respect for formal intellectual life" and thus "they rarely produce enduring intellectual insight."[39]

So where will Baylor get an understanding of the Christian faith sufficiently comprehensive to integrate with the intellectual life under-girding its comprehensive curriculum? Presumably from the "Big Three" Catholic, Lutheran, and Reformed traditions: perhaps Alvin Plantinga or Nicholas Wolterstorff in philosophy; Alasdair MacIntyre or Charles Taylor in ethics; George Marsden or Harry Stout in history; Mary Douglas or Peter Berger in the social sciences; John Polkinghorne or Arthur Peacocke in the physical sciences. But are the Christian perspectives of such scholars, as distinguished from their disciplinary research, detachable from the faith traditions in which they were nourished and then transferable to a quite different Baptist context? Intellectual life is profoundly ecumenical, scholars being trained to search for truth wherever it may be

---

[37] For a thoughtful expression of this concern see Robert M. Baird, "An Alternative Vision for Baylor," *The Baptist and Christian Character of Baylor*, edited by Donald D. Schmeltekopf and Dianna M. Vitanza with Bradley J. B. Toben (Waco, TX: Baylor University, 2003) 99-108.

[38] Mark A. Noll, "Is There a *Baptist* Theology in the House? A Review Essay," *Perspectives in Religious Studies* 28, no. 3 (2001): 285-90.

[39] Mark A. Noll, "Christian Higher Education and Southern Baptists: Hopeless or Hopeful?" *The Educator*, First Quarter (2004): 5-6.

found. But what happens when we try to transplant the kind of truth that has been shaped by distinctive worship practices, by a particular style of religious community, even by the memory of unique historical crises? How deeply can Baylor drink from wells dug by others and still retain its Baptist identity?

As with the evangelical paradigm at Union University, I leave each reader to evaluate the relevance of the establishment paradigm for Baylor University. Anyone who knows anything about the Baylor experiment will realize that I have chosen not to dwell on the bitter controversy that has dogged it from the beginning, not only because I have dear friends on all sides of the conflict, but because I think the approach should be judged on its merits rather than in terms of the personalities engaged in the sort of High Noon shootout that Texans seem to relish. Some lament top-down, heavy-handed administrative interference in faculty affairs while others insist that change of this magnitude requires the most aggressive possible initiatives by its sponsors. I only hope that Baylor is not trying to do in one decade what Notre Dame was able to accomplish in a half-century by building on 750 years of cumulative Catholic endeavor.[40]

CONCLUSION

What have we learned from these soundings regarding the present place of Baptists in the higher education dialogue? The first is that our colleges and universities have been so closely tied to the supporting churches and denomination that significant changes in the latter profoundly affect the former. Based on a wide-ranging study of Christian higher education, Robert Benne has concluded that "sponsoring churches... supply the persons, ethos, and vision that are needed to shape the identity of the school and guide its mission.... Without a strong religious tradition–usually a church–behind it, a college can have great difficulty maintaining its

---

[40] In evaluating the recent achievements of Notre Dame it is important to remember that they reflect the thirty-five year presidency of Theodore M. Hesburgh (1952-1987) unique for its durability and stability during one of the most turbulent periods in the history of American higher education. It was followed in close continuity by the presidency of Edward A. Malloy, whose term is scheduled to end in 2005, the two administrations spanning fifty-three years.

religious identity and mission."[41] Powerful internal influences are eroding Southern Baptist support of its educational institutions, which goes far toward explaining why they have been muted in terms of articulating a distinctive vision rooted in a Baptist ethos.

Second, in light of these trends it is not surprising to find that traditionally Southern Baptist schools are experimenting as never before with other models, especially the evangelical paradigm of a Wheaton and the establishment paradigm of a Notre Dame. If grassroots Southern Baptist leaders continue to neglect or even abandon the educational imperative of the Christian faith, we may well see even more trends in this direction despite the inherent difficulties of adapting an imported model to a Baptist context. At one extreme, the evangelical paradigm offers theological reassurances to the constituency but is so narrowly biblicistic that it offers a university faculty limited avenues of genuine intellectual integration. At the other extreme, the establishment paradigm is so comprehensive that it threatens to overwhelm the limited conceptual framework that Baptists have thus far developed in which to express the uniqueness of their faith. Some schools may seek to hybridize the two models, as Baylor has done to some extent, but this will not reduce the internal tensions that are likely to accompany the implementation of either approach.

Third, if the denomination does not reverse present trends by rallying behind its educational institutions, and if it proves difficult or even impossible to make models developed elsewhere truly indigenous to Baptist life, we will doubtless see even more of our schools cut their traditional Baptist ties. The first four who showed us how this might be done are all flourishing with a revised sense of mission. Those that remain tethered to their church-related tradition cherish the Baptist connection and are deeply grateful for the sacrificial support that they have received over many years. They will not forsake the denomination unless it first forsakes them. Some view the possibility of such separations as a betrayal[42] and seek

---

[41] Benne, *Quality with Soul*, 67.

[42] Charges of betrayal have long been popular in Baptist pulpits, such as the regular fulminations of W. A. Criswell against Baylor University, with blame being assigned almost invariably to the schools rather than to the churches for any rupture in their relationship. More recently this declension thesis has gained

to tighten the bureaucratic screws of coercive control, but that is no way to run either a denomination or a university. Instead, the denomination, in partnership with its schools, needs to develop a shared vision for higher education that both partners can enthusiastically support.[43] There is not much time left to prove that being Baptist is more of an asset than a liability to the cause of Christian higher education.

---

currency in scholarly discussion due primarily to George M. Marsden, *The Soul of the American University: From Protestant Establishment to Established Nonbelief* (New York: Oxford University Press, 1994); and James Tunstead Burtchaell, *The Dying of the Light: The Disengagement of Colleges and Universities from Their Christian Churches* (Grand Rapids: Eerdmans, 1998). On Baptist devolution in historical perspective see William H. Brackney, "Secularization of the Academy: a Baptist Typology," *Westminster Studies in Education* 24, no. 2 (2001): 111-28.

[43] Somewhat as a sequel to this essay, I plan to address the matter of a shared vision for higher education rooted in a Baptist ethos as part of a theme issue on "Forming Baptist Identity in American Higher Education: Challenges and Prospects" scheduled for publication in *Perspectives in Religious Studies*, Winter, 2005.

CHAPTER ELEVEN

The Radical Call to Service: The Five Tasks

By Mary Poplin
Claremont Graduate University

Twelve years ago, when I knelt down during a communion service in the tiny Methodist church my mother had grown up in, and said to God "Please come and get me" I was a radical. I was a full professor with tenure teaching structuralism, deconstructivism, critical theory, feminist theory, multiculturalism, and well on my way to post–modernism. If you had asked me about my calling, if I could have answered at all, I would have said it was to stay on the edge of new trends and apply them to education. So I went through one theory after another. Each time the search would end in boredom. I was constantly escaping boredom. One graduate tells me that I would tell students they could use any sources in their course papers except the Bible. I thought of myself as quite open–minded, of course. I also thought of myself as quite "spiritual," I was surfing the spiritual net in every arena, even bending spoons. The only place I would not look was Christianity. I believed all the professors I had who told me that Christianity was oppressive and the academy was no place for God. It hadn't occurred to me to look around the world and see where people were the least oppressed or to think that if there were a God who created the world and all that is in it, it would matter in the study of everything.

In my personal life, I had been a kind of Rahab and had the favor of the university, but soon after my conversion, I was to become something of a leper at the country club. I was to come to understand that Christianity, like any religion – from secular humanism to Buddhism – forms a worldview that holds implications not just for one's personal life but profoundly for the way one approaches one's academic discipline. I was also soon to learn that the radical diversity and academic freedom proclaimed by the university primarily favors the leftist and non-monotheistic worldviews. All academicians are religious about their convictions; the only difference is whether their convictions include the metaphysical, truth and/or God.

After three years of intense personal study of the Bible and encountering and learning from many in the incredibly diverse body of Christ, I took a sabbatical to work alongside Mother Teresa and the Missionaries of Charity for two months to understand why they said their work was not social work but religious work. Since my own work addressed the education of various marginalized groups I thought this would be one place to start to see how principles of Judeo-Christianity might relate to my own work.

Mother Teresa's work—and that of her Missionaries of Charity—was about as far from mine as one could get. I teach in an elite college town with all the comforts and conveniences. Their daily lives lived among the poorest of the poor (no returning to middle class neighborhoods at night) consisted of an endless sequence of praying, cleaning, cooking, washing, receiving visitors, and bathing and feeding people (usually very sick people). She and her sisters quickly provided those of us there with lessons in vocation/calling. First, we were to learn that their first work is not the actual activity with the poor; their first work is prayer. From prayer comes the will and the power to work in the streets. She said, "We take Jesus from the altar each morning (Eucharist) to meet Jesus in the distressing disguise of the poor on the streets."[1] Secondly, she said their work with the poor was not their vocation – their vocation was to belong to God and to become "holy." Third, she said God has many jobs to be done in the world, every one is not called to the poor; some are actually called to work with the wealthy (who she felt were often "spiritually the poorest of the

---

[1] The Scripture around which their work is formed is Matthew 25:35-36 where Jesus tells the disciples, "For I was hungry and you gave me food, I was thirsty and you gave me drink, I as a stranger and you welcomed me, I was naked and your clothed me, I was sick and you visited me, I was in prison and you came to me." All Scripture references are taken from the English Standard Version, 2000, Wheaton, IL: Crossway.

poor"), and/or to be wealthy themselves. She admonished everyone, "You have to find your own Calcutta."

When I returned from Mother Teresa's, I had a more thorough understanding of Christianity and now almost four years of experience trying to follow Christ. I knew Jesus was real, alive and actively working in, with and through everyone who believes and asks. He was no longer just another mythic or historic figure. I knew why God calls Himself, "I AM" and not "I was" or "I think." I understood why Augustine said "I believe in order that I may understand" because there were many things I could not even see, much less understand, until I believed. I knew that God had a different worldview on any subject that could be named – intellectually, socially, politically, psychologically, artistically, legally, scientifically and economically; and that His precepts, principles, perspectives and actions are more whole, connected and life-giving than any theory or philosophy the secular academy has ever proposed. And I knew that the academy was built more after Descartes' rendition of self and understanding "I think therefore I am" than Augustine's. My intellectual boredom was coming to an end—could anyone ever know fully the mind of God even in the small area of education in which I was working? Could any chemist, psychologist, neurologist, lawyer, philosopher, mechanic, mother or musician fully know Him and how His design and principles and life informed their work?

Upon my return from Mother Teresa's, I had an ever-increasing awareness as I taught that the only intellectual perspective I was leaving out in my courses was the Judeo-Christian one. I began to feel like a liar to my students or, at best, that I was hiding something from them for fear of embarrassment. While I do not believe it is my responsibility in the secular academy to provide students exclusively or even primarily the Judeo-Christian perspective unless the course is overtly directed toward it, I know leaving it out of any class is like withholding a critical option for viewing the world. I had never before left out any secular view or even religious view that I knew.[2] I had always prided myself on offering a wide range of views on the topics I was teaching though I was quite dogmatic

---

[2] I often had students read texts that were Buddhist, theosophist, and feminist theology.

about the ones I believed or disbelieved at any given moment. My intellectual crisis was full-blown, my Calcutta was taking shape.

STARVATION, ABSENCE, AND STAGNATION

As I became a more consciously Christian observer of the academy, three realities began to impress themselves upon me that have influenced the five tasks I will address in this essay. I began to see the starvation of students and faculty, the absence of the Judeo-Christian perspective at the table of ideas, and the stagnation of fields inside the university. The starvation of students manifests itself in many ways. Graduate students tend to be hungry for bigger pictures and enlarged understandings of the world, yet the reductionistic academy trains them in increasingly narrowed specializations, in the social sciences and humanities these narrowed specializations are also increasingly drawn from very narrow ideological stances.

Christian students who have been silenced in the academy long for even a single encouraging word in a class and someone with whom they can engage the Judeo-Christian worldview relative to the content they are being taught. Students who are not Christian sense a kind of emptiness that they, like me, try filling with many different things–exotic spiritual searches, antidepressants, drugs, alcohol, multiple relationships, busyness (jobs and school). They are particularly hungry for metaphysical experience and understandings. While this may make us uncomfortable because most of us have grown up in the academy post metaphysics of any kind, I am certain I could not have become a believer based solely on rationalized apologetics and explanations of God emerging from modernism. I need to know that Christ still heals, that God speaks in often inexplicable ways, and that we do not live in a purely natural or purely knowable world. I have to remain connected to the miraculous and constantly search for the still small voice or else my faith, my personal growth, and my intellectual work suffer. Separating the supernatural from the natural and even from the academic study of God drives students to other spiritualities and/or radical political movements. People know in their spirits there is more and are not so much afraid of the Christian walk being difficult as that it may be just one more boring philosophy of life.

Christianity must be distorted to make it either easy or boring. I also believe there is a concomitant starvation of faculty whether they are Christian or atheist that tends to manifest itself in frustration, depression, anger, jealousy, gossip, busyness, fear and feelings of insignificance in their lives.

Second, I began to see that the only worldview not represented at the academic roundtable is the Judeo-Christian one. I sometimes use a Scripture in class to explain a concept that is present or missing in the text or discussion we are having about education. It is then that I notice how many Christians there are in graduate school – heads are raised, eyes brighten and an occasional smile replaces the initial shocked expression. In a qualitative research class a few years ago one of the women graduate students presented a qualitative study she had read on three new evangelical Christian church movements. She did the usual presentation, describing the purpose of the study and the way the data had been gathered and analyzed, and the results reported. While she presented about these evangelical movements, several students rolled their eyes during the presentation as though the speaker herself might be presenting the text to mock the movements. A few other students, who I knew were Christians, were eager to hear about the text. At the conclusion of her presentation, three students spontaneously made derogatory personal comments, such as, "Oh, that's the church my ex-husband goes to" and "That church hates women." These comments gained the laughter and head-nodding of much of the class. The Christian students, with the exception of the woman presenter, lowered their heads and eyes. It just so happened that in "that church that hates women" this female student was to be ordained within a few weeks. Class had run overtime and I dismissed them. Increasingly uncomfortable during the week I decided to confront what had happened at our next meeting. I pointed out that if we believed that it was good for us to hear diverse points of view, it was good across the board and used a drawing on the board to demonstrate that none of us are quite as open-minded as we think we are.

While colleagues who represent Buddhist, humanist, atheist, naturalist, agnostic, new-age, feminist, critical, postmodern, liberal, Marxist, and other worldviews occupy seats with ease at the academic table of ideas, Christians do not. Even when we are seated there, we may be silent out of embarrassment and fear.[3] However, I believe primarily we are reluctant to engage the academic discourse because we have not done enough homework to have fully developed strong alternatives. Most of us have little experience and no training thinking in our disciplines through Judeo-Christian lenses at any real intellectual depth. Even students who come from Christian universities have rarely been taught rigorously to interrogate Christian versus secular principles in any disciplines.[4] The academy then is robbed of a critical worldview, one that is increasingly dominant in non-northwestern cultures.[5] These struggles to gain access to and engage the intellectual dialogue are intense and not without their controversies and real costs.

Lastly, I began to notice how my own discipline and related ones have become increasingly reductionistic and stagnated. In reality, there is very little difference between the graduate social-science classrooms today and those I attended in graduate school (even undergraduate school thirty years ago). We were liberal to Marxist then and the various forms of relativity were very much alive even though we didn't call them postmodern, we called them progressive. We questioned the missing texts of gender and culture groups but didn't yet call classical education the colonization of minds, but our professors had already abandoned it. The authors and vocabulary of the books have changed somewhat but the basic understandings, debated issues and core beliefs of the field have not. Education is thoroughly humanistic, liberal, and increasingly leftist and we are still operating as though some continued form of liberal social programming or radical Marxist critical theory will cure the educational problems of the poor. We won't teach the difficult subjects to students, especially students of color and the poor for fear of hurting their feelings (the liberal mindset) or colonizing their minds (the radical mindset).

---

[3] Hugh Hewlitt, *The Embarrassed Believer* (Nashville, TN: Word Publishing, 1998).

[4] I teach a class each summer that seeks to help students do this and some can and are eager to, but many who choose the class have not begun to understand even the most basic principles of Christianity. They have odd mixes of secular and Christian principles sitting side by side uncontested.

[5] See Philip Jenkins, *The Next Christendom* (Oxford: Oxford University Press, 2002).

Many teachers no longer have either the hope or the will to do the hard work it takes effectively to teach the poor. The ideologies teachers are taught are particularly ineffective and the resistance mounts, from elementary school to graduate school, to subject our work to hard measures of accountability.[6]

Sadly, I began to see that these problems of starvation, absence and stagnation were not unique to secular universities. Christian colleges are often equally enamored with the secular philosophies and thus are in similar, if not worse, condition. Worse because there is a hesitation in throwing oneself wholly into the secular and yet there often is not a concomitant rigorous intellectual engagement to sort it all out using Judeo-Christian principles. To do this will take a much more rigorous immersion in the Christian mind and Spirit and increasingly stronger walk with God. On the other hand, gratefully, God always calls us to tasks we cannot possibly do without Him and, after all, He has supplied us with the mind of Christ and His Spirit; what more could we need?

THE TASKS

It seems to me there are five interrelated tasks that Christian scholars must engage in order to serve in the university today. These include (1) seeking the mind of Christ and the Holy Spirit for our disciplines, (2) building a diverse community of Christian scholars around this task, (3) securing places at the academic tables, (4) increasing in holiness, and (5) serving students, colleagues and the university. I believe these five tasks are necessary in both secular and Christian universities and colleges. I fully recognize and respect the way God's calling on each of us differs and that there is an infinite set of possibilities for how He creates, molds and calls us. So these tasks are described from my unique experience over the past twelve years. All this is to say that one must read this mix of personal experience, Biblical and academic reference through one's own calling. It is my hope that there will be aspects of these tasks that will speak to and encourage others' unique callings.

---

[6] Mary Poplin and John Rivera, "Merging Social Justice and Accountability." *Theory into Practice* 44:1 (2005).

SEEKING THE MIND OF CHRIST AND THE HOLY SPIRIT

Once I really understood the connection between the first chapters of Genesis, John and Colossians, there was no longer any possibility of denying that God, Christ and His Spirit could not be excluded in any serious intellectual endeavor from science to education to art. Newman put it this way, "I only say if there be Religious Truth at all, we cannot shut our eyes to it without prejudice to truth of every kind, physical, metaphysical, historical and moral; for it bears upon all truth."[7]

In the beginning, it is revealed there were three (Elohim). There was God, there was His Spirit hovering, waiting on the third–the Word–to be spoken by God throughwhich all of creation came into being (Genesis 1:1-3). The Word, through whom all things were made, Jesus Christ, became flesh and dwelt on earth among human beings, the very incarnation of the Word of God spoken in the beginning (John 1:1-3). In Colossians (1: 15-17), Paul further instructs us, "Jesus is the image of the invisible God, the firstborn of all creation. For by Him all things were created, in heaven and on earth, visible and invisible, whether thrones or dominions or rulers or authorities–all things were created through Him and for Him. And He is before all things and in Him all things hold together." Because of this, without God any discipline is incomplete or as philosopher Dallas Willard summarizes, "Jesus is the smartest person in your field."[8]

I find the book of Daniel is particularly relevant for those of us in the academy. Daniel and his friends were young men who were determined by Chaldean royalty to be noble, beautiful, wise, knowledgeable,understanding and competent to stand before the king. They knew and honored God and though they served pagan authority they refused to break God's commandments. When taken into captivity they were educated for three years (about the length of time of graduate coursework) in all the literature and language of the Chaldeans (Daniel 1:4-5). We are told that at the end of their three years of secular education "in every matter of wisdom and understanding about which the king inquired of them, he found them ten times better than all the magicians and enchanters that were in all his

---

[7] John Henry Newman, *The Idea of a University* (Notre Dame: University of Notre Dame Press, 1982) 39.

[8] Dallas Willard, *The Divine Conspiracy* (San Francisco: Harper Collins, 1998).

kingdom" (Daniel 1:20). This is the potential of Christian scholars, unrealized as it may often be. William Craig suggests that many Christians "have for the most part been living on the periphery of responsible intellectual existence."[9]

Like Daniel, we are educated in all the secular world has to offer but we do not accept it as wholly true. This education, because it is absent its Creator, cannot be wholly true. We can all expect that inside all secular knowledge there will be distortions and false principles residing next to true ones and/or hidden things yet to be uncovered that will not be revealed without restoring God to the picture. Though even the most committed Christian scholar will fail to apprehend completely the whole truth of God, we can nonetheless be certain that there is a truth and it belongs to God and that He has given us ways to seek it. "It is the glory of God to conceal things, but the glory of kings is to search things out (Proverbs 25:2)."

I would suggest that scholars such as Robert George, David Aikman, Philip Johnson, Jean Bethke Elshtain, Kathy Bassard, Elizabeth Fox Genovese, James Hunter, Miroslav Volf, Charles Glenn, Dallas Willard, Carol Swain, Glenn Loury, William Dembski, Robert Sloan, Michael Behe, George Marsden, J. Budziszewski, Nancy Piercy, Fredericka Mathewes-Green, Armand Nicholi and many others have insights that are unique and invigorating to the academy because they have not limited their seeking to the secular academy. With God, whether overtly referenced or not, scholars have access to more wisdom than without God. And like C.S. Lewis said of Christians in general,[10] Christian academics may not necessarily be better academics but they will be better than they would be without God.

William Craig calls on Christian scholars to interrogate the very foundations of our various disciplines. He says, "As Christian academics we cannot afford to be unreflective and simply absorb uncritically the common presuppositions of our discipline, for these may be antithetical

---

[9] William Craig, *On Being a Christian Academic* (Addison, TX: Lewis and Stanley, 2004) 11. See also George Marsden. *The Outrageous Idea of Christian Scholarship* (Oxford: Oxford University, 1997) and Mark Noll. *The Scandal of the Evangelical Mind* (Grand Rapids: Wm. Eerdmans, 1994).

[10] C. S. Lewis. *Mere Christianity* (New York: Macmillan, 1952).

to a Christian *Weltanschauung*. As educated Christians our goal should be to have a Christian *Weltanschauung*, a world and life view that provides a Christian perspective on the arts, on physics on literature, on business, on poverty, on everything. All truth is God's truth, no area of study lies outside the domain of God's truth. Somehow it is all integrated into the whole, which is perfectly known by God alone. Our goal should be to seek to discover how our field of study fits into the whole scheme of God's truth."[11]

We must act in ways that will help us receive wisdom, knowledge, understanding and revelation regarding the mind of Christ in our various disciplines. Peter gives us a pattern to follow: "Make every effort to supplement your faith with virtue, and virtue with knowledge, and knowledge with self-control, and self-control with steadfastness, and steadfastness with godliness, and godliness with brotherly affection and brotherly affection with love" (2 Peter 1:5-7). These, we are told, will make us fruitful. It is critical as a Christian scholar to see that Peter sets the pursuit of knowledge behind the pursuit of faith and virtue and proposes that once we have knowledge we must also have self-control, perseverance, godliness, and love. It is not possible to separate faith and virtue from the pursuit of knowledge and become an effective or fruitful Christian scholar. Again, to believe is to be able to understand.

There are many aspects of seeking the mind of Christ and Spirit of God for our disciplines that I will not fully develop here. However, I will mention a few ways we can begin and some experiences I have had in my own fumbling toward engaging my own discipline. First and foremost, I believe scholars must thoroughly engage the entire Scriptures. I know that we can also study other texts about the Bible and Christianity but personally I believe the Scriptures are far more "living and powerful" and I have experienced that the Lord works powerfully with our minds as we engage them. Human explanations have too much doctrine and preference for or against emphasizing particular principles and precepts over others. Having engaged in the secular and "bohemian" lifestyle for so long, I was not even able to read Christian books for the first three years after my conversion, rather I was called to read Scriptures over and over, listen to

[11] Craig, 23, 18.

them on tape, and even to hand copy the New Testament, Psalms and Proverbs. During the time I was copying Scriptures, I could sometimes actually feel as though there was neural realignment going on inside my head as I wrote. I am not suggesting these activities for others. Unless one is really called by God to do so, it would become simply a "religious" activity yielding little or no fruit. But I am proposing that we begin to see the Scriptures as equally critical to the development of our knowledge of our fields as the latest academic journal.

What I am proposing is entirely different from Bible studies, sermons and homilies though these can help us in our personal walk with Christ. As scholars we must approach the study of Scripture as though it were a primary text of our discipline also. There is a Benedictine discipline that can help here–*lectio divina*. In *lectio divina*, monks and nuns pray before they read asking that the text would enter deeply into their spirits and souls and so transform them. They seek to be open and sensitive to any revelation God would want to give them. The process of this prayerful reading of Scripture is to pray, read, and meditate. I propose we do this not just for our personal lives but for actively seeking insights and revelations regarding the foundational principles and specific goals of our academic work.[12]

A few years ago, I kept asking for a Scripture to help me understand why all the attempts to teach social justice to our teacher interns weren't producing more effective teachers with the poor. I kept sensing that the Lord wanted me to study the adulterous woman Scripture. Given my past, I thought perhaps the Lord had forgotten I had moved on, but eventually after many readings I saw that in this passage, Jesus calls the community to be accountable for their sins first and second the woman herself. The community played a role in her sin and her healing. But, she was not told everything was okay, be on your way you poor child, you must have had a difficult childhood; she was told to go and sin no more. Like the community who had brought her to trial, first, educators must be held accountable for results of their students first and, secondarily, their

---

[12] Because I struggle with the discipline it takes to sit down and read through the whole Bible, I often use a one–year Bible. While I may be ahead or behind the specific date, I read it seeking particular things each year and note them.

students must be held accountable as well. We were, at that time, holding neither accountable. Still we see much resistance to the precepts of accountability for the education of the poor inherent in the "No Child Left Behind" legislation. I share these things to encourage us that the Biblical texts, like this parable, that we think we know so well hold so much more truth than we can imagine–revelation that can speak to our own disciplines. It is not that its surface meaning is not true, it is that there is even more truth for the diligent seeker. There are levels of truth in the Bible, precept upon precept, and every time we sit with it, it is the same but we are different and we are more or less ready to receive increasing levels of revelation.

Another principle frequently cited in the Hebrew Scriptures that I believe has significance for many of us, particularly in the humanities and social sciences, is the command not to turn to the left or the right.[13] Jesus never answered questions simply on the left (don't stone her) or on the right (stone her). While people often asked Christ yes/no questions, He never answered them in that way. His answers were always somehow both between and above that. The most revealing passage about the left and the right occurs in 1 Samuel chapters 5-7. Here the Philistines have stolen the ark, the very presence of God. After inhabitants of three cities are practically destroyed when the ark is placed in them, the Philistines decide to strap the ark to a cart led by two cows, never yoked, who are still nursing their calves. Still denying the facts set before them, the Philistines say IF the cows go toward Beth-Shemesh once the ark is loaded on them then we will believe that the God of Israel has brought these plagues on us because we have stolen the ark. And the Scripture says, "And the cows went straight in the direction of Beth-Shemesh along one highway, lowing as they went. They turned neither to the right nor to the left." The more of His presence the more straight will be our path.

Perhaps the reason the Lord quickened these left/right Scriptures to me is that I was so far to the left, when I became a Christian that I tended at first to move too far to the right. I was tempted to think all secular knowledge was untrue. But because evil cannot create, secular knowledge

---

[13] See also Joshua 1:7, Proverbs 4:27, Deuteronomy 2:27, 5:32, 17:11,20, 28:14, I Samuel 6:12.

frequently contains distortions, wrong mixes and omissions that lead to error. I believe these occur in the social sciences as a result of Christian disengagement from some very real problems at any given historical moment. The secular world then defines the problem and the solutions and because they are the only ones or first ones working on defining the problem and the solution, they win the day. Christians then are placed in the difficult and less productive intellectual position of contending with the secular rather than being out front with life-giving solutions. The multicultural agenda is a good example of this. Christian academics did not take up the very real issues of racism that plagued the nation, so we were left in a position of accepting/refuting the secular ideas. Christ's solutions to racism would be both far more radically demanding (much like His suggestion that even to look at a woman with lust is adultery) and more conservative (sifting the chaff from the wheat) than the modern and postmodern interpretations we have now.

In the first year of my walk with Christ, I attended a seminar led by Bill Gothard on the various ministry gifts. I went that week praying that the Lord would reveal to me if I were really called to be a teacher since that had been my entire career. I have taught from elementary school to graduate school. After the session on the teaching gifts, I had a very brief and wordless dream where *I was standing in the middle of a desert with nothing but sand around me and Christ appearing at first as a speck on the horizon walked up to me and drew a dove, the symbol of the Holy Spirit, on my forehead and then disappeared.* I awoke knowing, I was a teacher and I would struggle, as Gothard had warned, to keep my mind under His Holy Spirit. I believe that this dream is a prophetic dream indicating a problem with which many Christians in the academy struggle, keeping our minds under God's direction. There is such a draw intellectually to allow our minds to invent things that are stylish, clever, unique and over-rationalized. Our soulful minds and emotions become so wedded to them that we do not subject our thoughts to all the tests through the Word and the Spirit that we need to. The academy, journals and book publishers reward these distortions.

We must also allow the Holy Spirit to speak to us by setting aside our hardened rational impulses. God is more than the greatest mind. John of the Cross in the 1500s taught that the intellect unfired by faith would become distorted. "[I]t is by means of faith that the intellect is united with God.... Faith darkens and empties the intellect of all its natural understanding and thereby prepares it for union with divine wisdom."[14] We must be prepared to receive, through the Spirit of God, revelations that will shock our intellect out of the common distortions of our disciplines. Malik describes this process in the academic life,

> So there is a problem here; truth and knowledge cannot be alien to Jesus Christ, the Eternal Logos; and yet the more we know scientific and philosophic truth the more we seem to be alienated from him: the more we cling to him in love the more our intellectual grasp of scientific and philosophic truth appears to suffer and the less we can converse with the great minds on an equal footing. Mind and spirit appear to be two radically different worlds; they do not understand each other; they cannot communicate, let alone commune, with one another; they profoundly disturb one another; each wishes the other did not exist; each hates the sight of the other; each wishes to be left alone.... I can only say we must trust the mercy and love of Christ even in this impossible situation.[15]

Like in the dream, the Holy Spirit is the corrective to the over-intellectualizing and over-rationalizing Christian principles. I have more faith than Malik that the mind of Christ and Holy Spirit are uniquely fit together and that we are simply so well indoctrinated into naturalism and rationalism that we have lost the ability to be free in them. The Holy Spirit is what we often diminish (although I don't think we ever can get fully out from under the Holy Spirit as Christians) by avoiding such experiences as fully engaging in the act of worship, asking for and expecting miracles, and being in the presence and glory of God for periods of time. While we rarely discuss these things, the Asbury revivals are examples of how the Holy Spirit can and will act upon academic institutions and individuals.[16] Dennis Kinlaw, president of Asbury during this time said, "Give me one divine moment when God acts, and I say that moment is far superior to all the human efforts of man throughout the centuries." These encounters change us, renew us and strengthen us in

---

[14] John of the Cross. *The Collected Works of John of the Cross* (Washington, DC: Institute of Carmelite Studies, 1991) 285, 448.

[15] Charles Malik. *A Christian Critique of the University* (Waterloo, ONT: North Waterloo Academic Press, 1987) 99-100.

[16] Robert Coleman, Editor. *One Divine Moment: The Asbury Revival* (Wilmore, KY: Asbury College, 1995).

spirit, soul and body, including in our minds. We need to raise this issue as one that needs attention by Christians in the academy. The actions of the Holy Spirit are the evidence: Students who are seeking the supernatural and are sensitive to the spiritual realm need to have been engaged by the academy. For example, why has not the academy stepped up to study scientifically the miraculous events happening in Christendom rather than critique those who proclaim them?

The word faith, like Holy Spirit, often causes problems for us because both Christian and secular academics often use this to suggest that it needs to be (can be) separated from academic work.[17] Having been fully engaged in the secular academy for fifteen years before becoming a Christian, I can attest that every scholar has faith in something(s) that serves as a foundational belief(s) and that faith is rarely challenged and fully integrated into her work, even though often unconsciously so. Ours also should be fully integrated, although consciously so. I once had faith in many conflicting foundational beliefs and either I did not notice or refused to be bothered by their lack of coherence, even with one another. Paul describes my earlier condition well—"For although they knew God, they did not honor him as God or give thanks to him, but they became futile in their thinking and their foolish hearts were darkened. Claiming to be wise, they became fools" (Romans 1: 21-22). Even Christians have often accepted the assumption that there should be a separation of our "faith" from our academic work.[18] But our faith *and* our evidence reveal intellectual, psychological, economic, artistic, scientific and social principles that challenge current foundational beliefs and hold out possibilities for discovering new truths in our disciplines. There is more evidence for God than there is for any secular philosophy from Marxism to naturalism. It takes much less faith to believe in God than to believe in Marxism.

Let us answer the skeptics and agnostics who are not certain whether

---

[17] Gene Edward Vieth, "Baptist Brawl," *World Magazine*. September 4, 2004. Vieth shares here that part of the contest at Baylor where President Sloan is attempting to renew the Christian emphasis in academics is that its previous president holds that faith should be separated from academic work.

[18] George Marsden, *The Outrageous Idea of Christian Scholarship* (Oxford: Oxford University Press, 1997).

or not God exists with the fact that if God exists, then it must matter to everything. The answer to this question of God sets in course one's entire academic and intellectual life (and more).[19] Therefore, it cannot be taken lightly or viewed as some unnecessary question or issue of personal preference. It is the question for anyone seeking truth, knowledge, understanding and wisdom, whether they are modern, postmodern or Christian. John Henry Newman is eloquent here.

> Worse incomparably, for the idea of God, if there be a God, is infinitely higher than the idea of man, if there be man. If to blot out man's agency is to deface the book of knowledge, on the supposition of that agency existing, what must it be, supposing it exists, to blot out the agency of God? I have hitherto been engaged in showing that all the sciences come to us as one, that they all relate to one and the same integral subject-matter, that each separately is more or less an abstraction, wholly true as an hypothesis, but not wholly trustworthy in the concrete, conversant with relations more than with fact, with principles more than with agents, needing the support and guarantee of its sister sciences, and giving in turn while it takes: from which it follows that none can safely be omitted.[20]

There are many paths to seeking the mind of Christ and Spirit of God for our fields. Virtually all the spiritual disciplines can assist us once we have committed ourselves to being so informed. We engage Scripture and seek the mind of Christ and Spirit of God in ways that differ from other believers. There is no field that does not need this kind of interrogation and transformation. The rigor of this kind of seeking for our field is even more demanding than our traditional disciplinary study. Like Daniel, we will have to be masters of two languages and cultures. And like him, Jesus calls us also to live and engage in this world and not be taken in by it. Kathy Bassard likened Christians' work in the secular academy to that of the Jews in Babylon who in Psalm 137 are required to sing songs to their captors. She, like David, asks "How shall we sing the Lord's song in a foreign land?"[21]

---

[19] See for example Armand Nicholi, *The Question of God* (New York: Free Press, 2002).

[20] John Henry Newman, *The Idea of a University* (Notre Dame, IN: University of Notre Dame Press, 1982) 45.

[21] Kathy Bassard. *"Scripture Meditation: How Shall We Sing the Lord's Song in a Foreign Land* (aka Grab Your Harp)" (Berkeley, CA: C. S. Lewis Conference on

The natural world that we see and analyze by sight is not in Christianity the primary, first-order world, the spiritual is. And just like Daniel and many others we will feel the impact of what transpires in the spirit realm. Over and inside universities and disciplines there are worldviews in every discipline that have enjoyed many years of dominance. What appear often as unreasonable arguments, contestations, insults and unfortunate decisions are often consequences of challenges to strongholds of the mind with which the university has aligned itself. As Paul teaches we are not fighting the people who try to stop, humiliate or discredit us at the academic table, we are fighting what academics might call worldviews. For Biblical writers it was that and much more. "For we do not wrestle with flesh and blood, but against the rulers, against the authorities, against the cosmic powers of darkness, against the spiritual forces of evil in the heavenly places. Therefore take up the whole armor of God" (Ephesians 6: 12-13). "For though we walk in the flesh, we are not waging war according to the flesh. For the weapons of our warfare are not of the flesh but have divine power to destroy strongholds. We destroy arguments and every lofty opinion raised against the knowledge of God, and take every thought captive to obey Christ" (2 Corinthians 10: 3-6).

Without getting into some 'demon under every desk' doctrine that would allow us to avoid being responsible for our actions, I believe we need at least to lay out for engagement the idea that the kind of warfare described in Daniel will also happen to those of us called to the academy. We need to learn to work effectively against strongholds of the mind so that we do not simply interpret our troubles in soulish or emotional ways and respond to colleagues out of this same soulishness. Watchman Nee cautions us that

> We on the one hand usually consider emotion as soulish; consequently those who are easily moved or excited we normally categorize as soulish. On the other hand we forget that being rational does not at all constitute one as being spiritual. The misjudgment of spiritualizing a rational life must be guarded against equally as much as against that of mistaking a predominantly emotional life for spirituality.[22]

Academic Freedom, October 11, 2003).
[22] Watchman Nee, *The Spiritual Man* (New York: Christian Fellowship

These personal skirmishes or over-rationalizing conflicts will get us nowhere and most of the time will only serve to discredit us more and tarnish our witness. We have been given so much more, including the promise of being seated in heavenly places from whence we can begin to see and to fight the mindsets that need to be challenged in the timing and strategy of God, knowing all the while that we must be active and ultimately that the battle and the victory belong to the Lord. The academy in the U.S. and Europe is an extremely dominant force in shaping the entire world; when it promotes distortions and false ideologies, it produces global and catastrophic consequences. The battle in these high places is intense and we have been losing ground since shortly after the founding of the early colleges. Burtchaell detailing the disintegration of Christian colleges gives an example:

> Will Herberg asking his Christian friends why they had ever clung to such "a thinly Christianized version of the Greek ideal of intellectual self-realization....If man's good was the life according to reason, as it was in the classical-humanistic ideal, then a liberal education along academic lines was obviously appropriate; but how appropriate was it, indeed what sense did it make, if man's good was what the Christian faith must hold it to be–to know and do the will of God." [23]

THE BODY OF CHRIST

There are many things that separate us as Christians—denominations and doctrines in Christian churches; narrow disciplinary arrangements in universities; language differences, individualistic rewards and sanctions; and the racial, national and gender prejudices that exist in the world–but that is not the way God has designed the universe to function optimally. He designed it to function as a single body with Christ as the head. Therefore the full counsel of the mind of Christ is most readily accessible in community with other believers who have been given different gifts, callings, insights and abilities by birthright and experience. Only together do we make up the Body of Christ and God commands a blessing to be

---

Publishers, 1977) 18-19.
    [23] James Burtchaell. *The Dying of the Light* (Grand Rapids, MI: William Eerdmans Publishing, 1998) 821.

poured out on us when we "dwell in unity" (Psalm 133:3). He provides the best possibility for unity across peoples because *in* Him there is no Jew or Greek, slave or free, male or female. We will be most fully equipped to redefine our disciplines when diverse members of the body of Christ come together for the task, otherwise critical insights will be separated and lost to the whole body.

In the most extensive description of the Body of Christ, its diversity, and its proper functioning in Scripture (1 Corinthians 12) we are told, "For just as the body is one and has many members, and all are members of the body, so it is with Christ. For in one Spirit we were all baptized into one body–Jews or Greeks, slaves or free–and all were made to drink of one Spirit.... If the ear should say, 'Because I am not an eye, I do not belong to the body,' that would not make it any less a part of the body.... The eye cannot say to the hand, 'I have no need of you'.... On the contrary, the parts of the body that seem to be weaker are indispensable .... God has so composed the body, giving greater honor to the part that it lacked it, that there may be no division in the body, but that the members may have the same care for one another. If one member suffers, all suffer together; if one member is honored, all rejoice together." Martin Luther King Jr. put it this way to his fellow white citizens, "Until I am free to be who God created me to be, you will not be free to be who He has created you to be."[24]

In my own struggles to develop a new paradigm for the education of teachers for the poor and marginalized, I could never have come to the insight of combining social-justice imperatives with accountability without the help of a colleague, John Rivera, a Native American and Mexican-American, who has lived his life using these and other principles. These principles exist in the Scripture but they do not provoke or speak to me like they do him because of our differing experiences. It is one thing for me to voice the words but without a corresponding embodiment with a life, these words have no power—"faith without works is dead." White middle-class people, who have never had to seek God to confront racism,

[24] Clayborne Carson and Peter Holloran, Editors. *A Knock at Midnight: Inspiration from the Great Sermons of Reverend Martin Luther King* (New York: Warner Books, 1998).

cannot lead organizations or think tanks in productive ways to solve the dilemmas of race and culture. I am not suggesting there is no role for white middle-class people in this struggle, there are many, but they cannot do it alone and it cannot be done by simply proclaiming the words. While Rivera helped to lead our program, great strides were made to effect more productive and unique changes, form coalitions, move justice and accountability together. A few months after his departure the vision encountered renewed resistance and reverted to old paradigms of liberal social programming, diversity (undefined), and sentimentality. These have not in any way caused any great transformation in the educational outcomes of poor children. There are clearly more effective ways to educate the poor, but truly to merge social justice and accountability agendas, the dominant liberal to radical mindset must be replaced, and this will require incredible skill, commitment, perseverance, and even serious contestation.

The lessons of Babel and the upper room relate here. While people sought to build their own human tower to the heavens, God divided their languages and they were unable to communicate (Genesis 11). When they waited and sought Him together as one, He made them able to speak and hear in one accord the multiple languages of one another (Acts 2). The ivory tower with more akin to Babel needs to become the upper room filled with diverse Christian scholars speaking their different languages and hearing in one accord, seeking God for their disciplines. George Marsden warns us, "Contemporary Christian scholarship will not realize its potential unless it can establish a strong institutional base. Isolated individuals in university culture can make impressive efforts here and there, but unless their voices are concerted, they will be lost in the general cacophony of the contemporary academy."[25]

To seek the mind of Christ in biology, as in education, we will need not only biologists from all of His body—every race, tongue, and denomination—but also those outside of biology. Newman knew well the problems of increasing specialization where he predicted accurately that biologists would be called on to make ethical decisions they were not equipped to make. He writes,

---

[25] Marsden, 101.

I am assuming that there is reason and truth in the 'leading ideas,' as they are called, and 'large views' of scientific men; I only say that, though they speak truth, they do not speak the whole truth; that they speak a narrow truth, and think it a broad truth; that their deductions must be compared with other truths, which are acknowledged to be truths, in order to verify, complete, and correct them.[26]

The secular university's attempt to work in transdisciplinary ways is a weak but important move to address the problems Newman saw coming. But a group of diverse Christian scholars seeking individually and collectively the mind of Christ and Spirit of God on a particular topic or issue have far greater chances of making advances inaccessible by the secular academy. For example, we should have ten times greater opportunities to understand the true causes and cure for cancer, the solution to education for the poor, the economics most conducive to a just society. While Christian faculty fellowship groups exist on many campuses, they are rarely places for academically rigorous work, rather they are respites and havens to share meals and be encouraged in the company of other Christians in higher education. While havens are good and even necessary there is no reason why there cannot also be academically rigorous fellowships focused on particular disciplinary issues informed and encouraged by multiple Christian scholars from other disciplines, races, cultures and genders. God will surely bless the work of scholars representing His body.

TAKING A SEAT AT THE ACADEMIC TABLE

In early 2002, I had a dream that so clearly depicted the past and present state of the university that I offer it here.

In the beginning of the dream, I find myself in the basement of the colleges where I currently teach. The architecture is beautiful; it looks like the early gothic churches you find so much in Europe. I am amazed knowing that I have been at these colleges for 20 or so years and have never been in the basement. The basement is empty except for me. As I am walking and admiring the hallways, I suddenly hear sirens and fire trucks careening to a halt outside and the firefighters are yelling, "We have to find the terrorists." I think to myself they must be between here and the first floor and I raise my eyes and see a red silk fabric running the length of the ceilings in the basements. I wonder if the terrorists are hiding there. Then, I remember I am

---

[26] Newman, 71.

late for a faculty meeting and I go to find the steps to get up to the first floor, but all the steps are nothing but rubble, broken down and the entrances to the first floor are blocked. At last I see a light at the top of the rubble of one set of stairs about three feet long by one foot high and I believe that if I can climb up on my hands and knees I can dig myself out, which I do. Once in the faculty meeting, I sit and begin to listen. The president is proclaiming something I believe is completely untrue relative to Judeo-Christian principles (though I do not recall exactly what was being said). I suddenly am struck with the feeling of imminent danger and I say to a Jewish woman colleague next to me "we have to get out of here" and I awake.

Who could have predicted that the foundational worldview of Judeo-Christianity upon which and for which most early universities were founded would be so broken off from the mainstream university that it would be found knocking outside, an unwelcome guest only a few hundred years later (in most cases it was much less)?[27] Who else besides Christian scholars will open the door, lift up the gates, raise up former places of desolation, and reclaim a seat at the academic roundtable?

It is not enough to receive from God new insights in our field and keep them in our Christian fellowships; we must engage the very mind and spirit of the academy. Gaining access inside the secular university is a daunting task. First, we must be invited or invite ourselves to the table. Secondly, we must have the courage to propose new insights, challenge foundational assumptions, and ask new questions in the midst of colleagues who may eye us as suspicious, at best, irrelevant or even dangerous, at worst. We are not called as academics or as Christians to censor intellectual insights from students or colleagues. The diversity and strength of the academy is diminished by our silence. While insights that are specifically Judeo-Christian do not always demand they be identified as such, they generally will cause disruption because they threaten well-established mindsets. We only have to look at the controversies and the attempts to block publication and teaching of intelligent design theory[28] and the problems more conservative voices[29] have in the academy to see the costs.

---

[27] Burtchaell, *The Dying of the Light*.

[28] Richard Monastersky. "Biology Journal Says it Mistakenly Published Paper that Attacks Darwinian Evolution." *The Chronicle of Higher Education* 51, 3 (2004).

[29] Jennifer Jacobsen, "Conservatives in a Liberal Landscape," *The Chronicle of Higher Education* 51, 5 (2004).

While seeking God's precepts and working in diverse academic communities to address discipline based conundrums is prerequisite, having the courage to speak up at the academic table is far more challenging to our soul for it is not simply an intellectual task. The strength of our relationship with God and the degree of our commitment to reintroducing the foundational truths inherent in a Judeo-Christian worldview into the academy are directly proportional to our courage. Speaking at the table requires considerable grace and strength from God to risk persecution. Paul tells the Philippian believers (1:28-29) "[Do] not be frightened in anything by your opponents.... For it has been granted to you that for the sake of Christ you should not only believe in him but also suffer for His sake." While I am not really comfortable discussing suffering as a requirement for Christian academics, I think my reluctance is more out of fear of embarrassment than out of truth. Americans do not talk much about the suffering Scriptures, but it will surely happen and we can be assured that God has made a provision for all the grace that is necessary.[30] The challenge to occupy seats inside the academy is that we will very likely face persecution that even our persecutors will not understand. The vicissitudes of academic life as a Christian would have been difficult to predict even two hundred years ago when Judeo-Christianity was the foundational truth upon which the very university was founded. Marsden suggests a reason for this: "There were no well-developed schools of Christian academic thought outside the field of theology itself. The Christian heritage was thus relatively easy to undermine academically."[31] The grace, strength and even suffering given us as Christian academics will exercise and both build our faith and deepen our understanding of God and of the world into which we inquire.

HOLINESS

I shudder to think how unqualified I am to write this section of the five tasks and know there are many far more qualified to teach us on the pursuit of holiness. In my own life, I have many struggles and fail much of the

---

[30] Brother Yun with Paul Hattawy, *The Heavenly Man* (Mars Hill, London: Monarch Books, 2002).

[31] Marsden, 16.

time. I write it though because I know God is calling us as Christians, in general, and specifically as Christians in the academy to come up to a higher level in our relationship with Him. It is He who will increase our faith and our hunger for Him and for His righteousness (Matthew 6:33). It is a necessary requirement for all the other tasks.

Mother Teresa said that the commonality among callings lay in only two areas. We are all called to belong to God and we are all called to be holy, to follow the life of Jesus. In order to be an effective Christian scholar we will have to grow more and more in communion with God, from whence all our help and wisdom come. The practice of spiritual disciplines of all kinds—worship, praise, various forms of prayer, silence, fasting, and study—is essential to our being able to seek the mind and Spirit of God. Dallas Willard writes, "If we are to succeed in 'putting off the old person and putting on the new,' then, or in having the mind or inner character of our Lord, we must follow an order of life as a whole that is appropriately modeled after his.... Our plan for a life of growth in the life of the kingdom of God must be structured around disciplines for the spiritual life."[32] This is not simply an intellectual task because in God there are no abstract, neat divisions to be had. Of all worldviews, His is the least reductionistic. The intellect, the emotions, the will, the spirit, and the body are all intricately connected and must all be continually purified. We will not be able to be continually immersed and enamored with the world and be able to locate new insights in our disciplines. This process of the call to holiness will differ among us, but, if we want, God will gradually remove us more and more from the pleasures of the world and give us the pleasures of His kingdom so that we can truly walk in the world and not be of it. Mother Teresa told me that she only sent the strongest of sisters to America because the comforts and entertainments of our culture were so alluring as to draw us away from God and from the knowledge of our dependence on Him. Like Daniel, there are things we simply cannot do and remain in fellowship with God.

When we are angry, unforgiving, anxious, fearful, or engaged in too much worldliness it affects our academic work and interactions with others

---

[32] Dallas Willard 352. See also Dallas Willard, *Renovation of the Soul* (Colorado Springs: NAVPress, 2002).

around us. Virtue precedes knowledge and the fear of God precedes wisdom, understanding and knowledge. The mind, the will and the emotions are the battlegrounds of our own soul. When out of order, they block access to walking, thinking, reading and being in the Spirit of God. We cannot be all God has called us to be intellectually until we are also following Christ with all our might, including yielding not only our minds but also our wills and emotions. There are many more qualified from every Christian tradition who have written on the pursuit of holiness, becoming like Christ, from the early fathers and mothers of the church and great revivalists to contemporary scholars.

MINISTRY TO STUDENTS AND COLLEAGUES

More than any other task, direct ministry to students and colleagues differs between the secular and Christian professors. Often Christian colleges have this as one of their missions, while secular colleges do not. Here again, many are more qualified than I to address this issue. I think particularly of times when I have heard Ken Elzinga of the University of Virginia speak on the topic.[33] We are called to be good professors and to contribute to our departments as much as we can and to serve our students to the best of our abilities.

In order to be the most effective professors we must be well-prepared, current, broadly educated, and actively engaged in our disciplines so that our teaching is relevant and current and our assistance to students in their own research is of the highest quality. I know that I am called to present fairly many worldviews on education; students need to know the range of ideas available to them, including the Judeo-Christian and Marxist worldviews. I need to prepare a place where students can read Aristotle, Augustine. E. D. Hirsch and Paulo Freire in the same space and discuss them. I need to show them the historic range of ways different generations from Socrates to the Middle Ages, Enlightenment, modern and postmodern times have conceived and implemented education. I want them to be able to distinguish the differences in the underlying principles, the problems, the advantages and the effects these various worldviews have

---

[33] Kenneth Elzinga, "*Jesus, the Master Teacher*," Los Angeles, UCLA: C. S. Lewis conference, 2001.

on education today. Because of the starvation I see in Christian students, I teach in the summers an elective class where we specifically explore worldviews since the Enlightenment (e.g., existentialism, postmodernism, and structuralism) as compared to the Judeo-Christian principles and precepts.

We are also called to contribute to the health of our departments to the best of our ability. Daniel, Joseph, Esther and many others served secular authority with excellence. Whether we are called to lead or to follow, we must do so with integrity, seeking the best for the department or school in which we work.

I am also very aware that there are many ways we are called to help students outside of just the academic when they seek us out. Sometimes this is simply to pray for them unbeknownst to them when they share with us their pain, losses and grief. Some students come to my office specifically for prayer or to request prayer because they have heard I will pray with them. Sometimes our call is to encourage them when they get stuck by going one step beyond what is required—help them search for what they need, shape their arguments, loan our books, meet them for a meal, or assist them in editing. And, yes, sometimes, when students ask, we are called to share our own stories.

LAST THOUGHTS

We are fortunate to be in the academy in a time when there is so much for a Christian scholar to do. A friend once showed me a video of Pastor Juanita Bynum preaching on God's callings. She said—"Your calling is in your tribulation." As frustrating as it is to be in the academy that has almost succeeded in removing any trace of its Christian foundations and quite effectively silenced its advocates, yet, what better time is there for us to live? And who besides us has been given so much access to the very substance and being from which all that we study is created? Let us then run the race with joy, peace and grateful hearts, with His Word and Spirit before us, and His wisdom, strength, courage, and grace propelling us forward.

Afterword

By Jean Bethke Elshtain
Laura Spelman Rockefeller Professor
of Social and Political Ethics
The University of Chicago

In 2002 I published an intellectual biography entitled *Jane Addams and the Dream of American Democracy*. Living intimately with the great reformer for a number of years, trying to "get inside" her complex life, I recognized very early on that Jane Addams's life was framed by Christian notions of a "calling" or a "vocation" and of one's life journey as a "pilgrim's progress." Such ideas were part of the cultural air that she breathed. You could no more escape calling, vocation, or pilgrimage than you could fly to the moon in 1889, the year Jane Addams and a childhood friend founded the extraordinary establishment known as Hull-House. For over nine years Addams had struggled with the question—what am I do to with my life?—and she had floundered, caught in what she called "the snare of preparation." A moment of revelation opens a clear pathway for her, she tells us, when she glimpsed in the half-light on a London evening "myriads of hands" grasping for cast-away, rotting vegetables. Witnessing the lives of the East End poor, the human flotsam and jetsam spewed forth by the harsh realities of the industrial revolution, Addams's pilgrimage became more sure-footed. She never looked back.

Calling, vocation, pilgrim's progress, revelation, witnessing: You cannot understand the life of this extraordinary woman unless you have a grasp of these understandings deeded to us by Christianity. That no doubt explains why so much of what is written about Jane Addams falls wide of the mark. Such understandings are quite simply unintelligible to a wide swath of our educated elites, not exempting a significant portion of the Christian clergy. So people apply Marxist or post-modern or structuralist or some other methodology or approach to Addams, busily deconstructing her own self-understanding, psychologizing her concepts, reducing her accomplishments to the terms of psychic need or political exigency. Of course, our psychologies enter in to what we do. And we are never outside a world of politics. But why the rush to sever a life from the understandings that give that life its meaning and purpose? Two reasons, I suspect: The first is ignorance and unintelligibility and the second, more unsavory, perhaps, is open hostility to religiously grounded understandings of a "self," past or present.

Addams had been educated at Rockford Seminary for Women, later Rockford College, in Illinois. The redoubtable head mistress of this institution energetically recruited educated, capable young women for the mission field. Addams resisted this call and disliked an overly intense religiosity. At the same time, this was a woman who, as a school-girl of sixteen, could write on the fly-leaf of a fellow student's school annual, "Life's a burden, bear it./Life's a duty, dare it./Life's a thorn-crown? Wear it/And spurn to be a coward." As I note, "A young woman who expresses such sentiments has not been reared on a diet of literary pap."[1] She, like the protagonist, Christian, of Bunyan's classic, takes the more arduous course.

Fast forward to the year 2005. Think about how we educate, how we teach, how we learn. Consider how rapidly we are losing, indeed, in many cases have lost, the ideas that framed Jane Addams' life and drove her on to higher purpose. A "career" is not the same thing as a "calling." A "job" is not identical to a vocation. A "career path" is scarcely the equivalent of a "pilgrimage." Now there are many in our midst who would say, in effect, "Why all the fuss? Career, job, career path—these are just different ways of talking about the 'same' things." Are they? No, indeed. For our concepts do structure the realities of our lives and our understandings. To the extent that we lose a rich vocabulary of calling and what it means to take one's stand on a given ground, we lose a particular sense of self. If the person suffering such self-loss (without knowing it, in many instances) is a teacher, he or she will view students differently as well. The lens of a "calling" underscores a view of students that thinks of the educations they receive as a form of moral formation—whatever the subject matter being

[1] Jean Bethke Elshtain, *Jane Addams and the Dream of American Democracy* (New York: Basic Books, 2002) 42.

taught in a particular classroom.

Over the years I have had students approach me—after they have spent a week or two in one of my classes—and state something along these lines: "I don't dare take this course. This stuff is so interesting and it gets me thinking in ways that don't fit into my career plans." Such students are often torn and their comments are not matter-of-fact. But they have been taught to think of "professionalization." They take workshops on how to succeed and how to work-the-system. As a result, they fear courses that require of them that they probe deeper, think harder, tackle troubling questions. It is a testimony to just how many of today's students are not afraid in this way that courses taught by teachers who exemplify a joy of learning tied to a calling are so frequently over-enrolled.

But one cannot help but notice something interesting and rather sad at the same time. For a good portion of such committed students, the course takes on a remedial quality. They are filling in gaps. They have never considered such ideas before. They do not have ready access to the biblically shaped language that was always on Jane Addams's finger-tips, even though she can by no means be called a creedal Christian in the full sense of the word. A few years back in a graduate seminar I offered at the University of Chicago we read a wonderful book by the British writer, P. D. James, whose own prose is profoundly shaped by the exquisite *Book of Common Prayer*, with its bold use of the English language to praise, to worship, to enjoin, and, it must be said, to chastise and, in some instances, condemn. One of the characters in this book, a woman who plays a key role in rescuing a baby about to be born and, then, as a new-born, from death, is called "Miriam." I said something to my students along these lines, "Of course, we know the background reference P. D. James is bringing to bear here. She taps into a powerful story familiar to nearly everyone." But I saw lots of perplexed faces before me. Not a single student could reach down and grasp the story of Moses' sister and the part she plays in rescuing her baby brother as he floated downstream.

This may not seem like such a "big deal," and perhaps not knowing Miriam straight off is not. But this loss of a point of reference speaks to deeper losses we have incurred. When one reads Abraham Lincoln's great speeches and the language of prophecy and of divine inscrutability and judgment ("God has His own purposes" and the Civil War as a punishment for slavery), and one appreciates that all Americans, north and south, had access to this language, one is reminded that how we think and in and through what categories, profoundly shapes how and what we understand. Bear in mind that when I speak of education, and of a "career" rather than a "calling," I am condemning no one. Many great teachers, including the overwhelming majority of my own mentors, were religiously agnostic or non-Christian. Yet they understood—they had access to—the reference points. My worry is that we are approaching, in much of higher education, a kind of cultural amnesia on many questions given our loss of certain understandings.

The relationship between faith, reason, and learning is a complex one and always has been. A simplistic fideism won't do, any more than a resolute bracketing of all concerns labeled "spiritual" or "religious." By that I mean that a teacher in the humanities who is areligious or even contemptuous of religious belief, and there are many, should still have access to a repertoire of concepts and understandings that help many students to make sense of their lives and their purposes. That this is not the case too frequently is attested to by the fact that many students report going underground, so to speak: They work to "fit in" and to speak the dominant language. They do not reveal what really drives them and gives them meaning. It isn't only teachers who leave no space for them—it is fellow students, at least at many of our elite institutions. The testimonies to this are, by now, so frequent and so often riddled with sadness and even anger, that no one should doubt it.

This is where the person with a calling, teaching joyfully, can be of such service by displaying the ways in which what St. Augustine called "faith seeking understanding" helps to make our worlds richer and more complex. We ill serve our students if we continue to wallow in the discredited "progressive hypothesis" that dictated that every successive epoch in the West would give rise to a higher level of "scientific" and "secular" reason, as religion faded into a discredited backdrop. This has not happened. Not only has it not happened but religions are on the rise around the world. Alas, some of the manifestations of religion are deadly and dangerous. It is, in many ways, a harrowing moment because the teacher with a calling is obligated to demonstrate the ways in which religion most of the time enriches rather than makes ignorant; the ways religion opens up the mind rather than closing it down; the ways religion promotes charitable interpretation of the lives of others, rather than seeing in those who do not share one's particular version of a particular faith only "infidels" who must be murdered or beaten back. That some versions of religion are intolerant and lead to terrible things means that those imbued with the joy of teaching and learning have an even greater weight on them than they would in less perilous times.

Students also need instruction on how to speak to those who do not share their categories, who do not participate in their understandings, who cannot penetrate their world of meanings. For we are all children of God; all flawed and groping; all yearning for a decent world. Those with a calling also have an obligation. The excellent volume you have completed reading alerts you to both the joys and complexities of "living out one's calling in the twenty-first century academy." Now more than ever we require those who, in the words of Robert Bolt's St. Thomas More, from the play, *A Man for All Seasons*, "serve God wittily, in the tangle of their minds."

Contributors

David Bottoms is John B. and Elena Diaz-Verson Amos Distinguished Chair in English Letters and Associate Dean for Fine Arts at Georgia State University in Atlanta. He earned his B. A. degree at Mercer and the Ph. D. from Florida State University. His first book, *Shooting Rats at the Bibb County Dump*, was chosen by Robert Penn Warren as winner of the 1979 Walt Whitman Award of the Academy of American Poets. His poems have appeared widely in magazines such as *The Atlantic, The New Yorker, Harper's, The New Republic, Poetry*, and *The Paris Review*. Dr. Bottoms is the author of four other books of poems, *In a U-Haul North of Damascus, Under the Vulture Tree, Armored Hearts: Selected and New Poems*, and *Vagrant Grace* as well as two novels, *Any Cold Jordan* and *Easter Weekend*. He is also coeditor of *The Morrow Anthology of Younger American Poets*. He is a founding coeditor of *Five Points*. In 2000, Governor Roy Barnes appointed him Georgia Poet Laureate.

R. Alan Culpepper is the founding dean of the McAfee School of Theology at Mercer University (1996). Prior to coming to Mercer, Alan taught New Testament at Southern Baptist Theological Seminary in Louisville, Kentucky (1974-1991) and at Baylor University in Waco, Texas (1991-1995). His writings reflect a sustained interest in the Gospels, especially the Gospel of John: *The Johannine School* (Scholars Press, 1975), *Anatomy of the Fourth Gospel* (Fortress, 1983), *John the Son of Zebedee: The Life of a Legend* (1994), "The Gospel of Luke," *New Interpreter's Bible*, vol. 9 (Abingdon, 1996), *The Gospel and Letters of John* (Abingdon, 1998). Currently, Alan is working on a commentary on the Gospel of Mark for the Smyth and Helwys Bible Commentary. In 2002, Mercer University Press published Alan's biography of his father: *Eternity as a Sunrise: The Life of Hugo H. Culpepper*, which chronicles his father's life and thought through his career as a missionary, prisoner of war, and professor of missions and world religions. Alan grew up in Chile and Argentina and received his education at Baylor University (B.A. 1967), Southern Baptist Theological Seminary (M.Div. 1970), and Duke University (Ph.D. 1974).

John Marson Dunaway is Professor of French and Interdisciplinary Studies at Mercer University and Director of the Mercer Commons (A Center for Faith, Learning, and Vocation). Educated at Emory (B.A. 1967) and Duke Universities (M.A., Ph.D. 1972), he is the author of six books and numerous articles, primarily on French religious writers of the twentieth century, including Julien Green, Jacques Maritain, Simone Weil, Georges Bernanos, François Mauriac, and Vladimir Volkoff.

Jean Bethke Elshtain is a political philosopher whose work shows the connections between our political and our ethical convictions. She is the Laura Spelman Rockefeller Professor of Social and Political Ethics at the University of Chicago. She has taught at the University of Massachusetts, Vanderbilt University and has also been a Visiting Professor at Harvard and Yale. She holds nine honorary degrees and in 1996 was elected a Fellow of the American Academy of Arts and Sciences. She has authored and/or edited twenty books—several having won awards—and written some five hundred essays. Professor Elshtain was born in the high plains of Northern Colorado and grew up in the village of Timnath, Colorado, population 185. Her journey has taken her all over the world but she remains, in many ways, a daughter of the high plains where she grew up among people who were hard-working, forthright and dedicated to their families, friends and community. Professor Elshtain has also received the Ellen Gregg Ingalls Award for excellence in classroom teaching–the highest award for undergraduate teaching at Vanderbilt University. In 2002, she received the Goodenow Award of the American Political Science Association, the Association's highest award for Distinguished Service to the Profession. In 2005-2006, Professor Elshtain will deliver the prestigious Gifford Lecturers at the Universities of Edinburgh.

R. Kirby Godsey has served as the seventeenth president of Mercer University since July 1, 1979. Prior to that appointment, he served as executive vice-president and as dean of the College of Liberal Arts. Before coming to Mercer in 1977, Dr. Godsey was vice-president and dean of the college at Averett University in Danville, Virginia. He is a graduate of Samford University and holds M.Div. and Th.D. degrees from New Orleans Baptist Theological Seminary, an M.A. in philosophy from the University of Alabama, and a Ph.D. in philosophy from Tulane University. The University of South Carolina, Averett and Samford have awarded him honorary degrees.

Dr. Godsey is the author of *When We Talk about God, Let's Be Honest* and has written numerous articles for scholarly and professional journals and denominational publications, including the *Journal of Higher Education*, *The Educator*, *The Journal of Philosophy* and *The Student*. He is active in the American Association of Higher Education and the American Philosophical Association. Dr. Godsey is a member of the Board of Directors for the National Association of Independent Colleges and Universities, for which he formerly served as a commissioner on policy analysis. He is a member of the Board of Trustees for the Southern Association of Colleges and Schools and has served the organization as a consultant-evaluator. A former president of the Georgia Foundation for Independent Colleges, Dr. Godsey frequently serves as a consultant and lecturer on topics related to higher education.

Jeanne Heffernan is a member of the Department of Humanities and Augustinian Traditions at Villanova University. She received an M.A. and a Ph.D. in Government from the University of Notre Dame, where she served as the associate director of the Erasmus Institute, a center dedicated to research in the intellectual traditions of the Abrahamic faiths. Prior to her appointment at Villanova, she served on the faculty of Pepperdine University. Trained as a political scientist, Professor Heffernan's primary research field is political theory, though her interests are interdisciplinary. She has lectured and published articles on Christian political thought, democratic theory, and faith and learning. She is currently editing a book on Catholic and Protestant contributions to the debate on civil society.

Richard T. Hughes is Distinguished Professor of Religion at Pepperdine University and Director of the Pepperdine Center for Faith and Learning. His books include *Models for Christian Higher Education* (ed. With William Adrian), *The Vocation of a Christian Scholar: How Christian*

Faith Can Sustain the Life of the Mind, and *Myths America Lives By*.

William E. Hull is Research Professor at Samford University where he previously served as Provost (1987-96) and University Professor (1987-2000). For more than two decades he served on the faculty and administration of Southern Baptist Theological Seminary. Hull is the author of "John" (*Broadman Bible Commentary*), *Love in Four Dimensions*, *Beyond the Barriers, Southern Baptist Higher Education: Retrospect and Prospect*, and contributor to numerous other books and periodicals.

David Lyle Jeffrey is Distinguished Professor of Literature and Humanities and Provost at Baylor University. Jeffrey is general editor and co-author of *A Dictionary of Biblical Tradition in English Literature* (1992). Among his other books are *The Early English Lyric and Franciscan Spirituality* (1975); *By Things Seen: Reference and Recognition in Medieval Thought* (1979); *Chaucer and Scriptural Tradition* (1984); *English Spirituality in the Age of Wesley* (1987; 1994; 2000); *The Law of Love: English Spirituality in the Age of Wyclif* (1988; 2001); and *People of the Book: Christian Identity and Literary Culture* (1996). In 1990, with Brian J. Levy, he published a critical edition with accompanying translations from the medieval French, *The Anglo-Norman Lyric*, and in 1999, with Dominic Manganiello, he edited and co-authored *Rethinking the Future of the University* (1999). In 2003 he published his latest book on biblical literature and its critical tradition in literary and cultural theory, *Houses of the Interpreter: Reading Scripture, Reading Culture*.

Gordon Johnston is Associate Professor of English at Mercer University, where he teaches courses in contemporary literature and creative writing and directs the Georgia Poetry Circuit. A former journalist, his poems, essays, and stories have appeared in *American Fiction, The Georgia Review, Atlanta Review, Denver Quarterly, Many Mountains Moving, Fourth Genre*, and other journals.

Mary Poplin is a professor of education at Claremont Graduate University. Her academic writing includes work on social justice, accountability, learning theory and pedagogy, research inside schools, teacher education and special education. She became a Christian in 1993 and has since sought to apply principles of Christianity in addressing the contemporary issues of education. In 1996, she spent two months working with Mother Teresa and the Missionaries of Charity in Calcutta to understand why she called her work "religious work not social work." For fourteen of the past twenty years, Poplin developed and directed the teacher education internship program at Claremont and was dean of the school from 2002-2004.

Jack L. Sammons is the Griffin B. Bell Professor of Law at Mercer University School of Law where he teaches First Amendment, Evidence, and Legal Ethics. The author of over forty articles, books, plays, poems and videos on a variety of topics relating to the practice of law, he was a founding member of the Chief Justice's Commission on Professionalism, the Georgia Judicial Campaign Ethics Committee, and he currently serves as Vice Chair of the State Bar of Georgia Formal Advisory Opinion Lecture. Professor Sammons is a Eucharistic Minister at St. James Episcopal Church in Macon, Georgia.

Andrew Silver is an Associate Professor of English at Mercer University. His book, *Southern Humor and Cultural Crisis* (2005), has been published by Louisiana State University Press, and his work has appeared in *Mississippi Quarterly*, *Prospects*, and *Legacy*. With the aid of the Mercer Commons, he published a documentary play, *Combustible/Burn* (2002) about a small group of devout students who helped end segregation at Mercer University in the 1960's. He lives in Macon, Georgia, with his wonderful wife and colleague, Anya, and his son, Noah Samuel.

Charlotte Thomas is Chair of the Philosophy Department of Mercer University, and an Associate Professor of Philosophy and Interdisciplinary Studies. A 1989 graduate of Mercer, she returned to teach at her alma mater in 1994. She lives in Macon, Georgia, with her husband Edward Thomas, who is also a member of the Philosophy Department at Mercer, and her two children, Francis and Isaiah.